D0049545

MAKE A TIKTOK EVERY DAY

DAVE JORGENSON

CONTENTS

We are a newspaper.

Quarantine
Day 210

The phrase "healthy addiction" may be fictional. What, after all, is healthy about an obsessive behavior? Still, if there are healthy addictions, and they make you and others happy, then creating TikToks must fall under that umbrella.

Since I began creating TikToks in May 2019, I haven't been able to stop. The questions people most often ask are, "Do you run out of ideas?" and "Are you ever worn out?" (the answers: no, and yes, of course, but I love it). When people take joy in what you're creating, and that creation is the result of your own creative process, it's hard to stop.

At the least, TikTok allows you to create something original and new every single day. At the most, TikTok allows you to create something original and new every single day—and get millions of free Internet points and views. Finding the motivation to stick with it 365 days a year is easy when you're having so much fun.

Have fun reading these prompts and remember: it just takes 15 seconds to make a 15-second TikTok.

INTERVIEW WITH

LOZCLAWS
(@Lozclaws)

Dave How did you first hear about TikTok?

Liz When videos from TikTok first came up on YouTube and it was more cringe compilations than anything. I remember I joined a Facebook group called "The people of TikTok must be stopped."

Dave You started on the Resistance side!

Liz I know! I was like, "This is so stupid. I'll never get it." And then my friend says, "I almost have ten thousand followers on TikTok ... for yodeling." So I joined TikTok to follow her.

Dave What is your process?

"I find if I plan things, I'm not funny... If I were to sit and think about things, nothing would get done."

Liz It just kind of pops up. Like Mother Nature *[a recurring character in her videos]*. I just picked up my phone and went back and forth. It's just me doing a transatlantic, overly annunicating woman, and also an amplified version of Liz that's just sick of everyone's stuff. I was born with a speech impediment so sometimes I have to redo my takes. I speak very, very quickly, which is now kind of on brand for me. I don't really refilm that anymore.

Dave My assumption was you just did that to fit things into 60 seconds.

Liz No-I-speak-so-quickly-Dave-you-have-no-idea-Jersey-Italian. Most of Mother Nature is ad-libbed. I find if I plan things, I'm not funny. I don't consider myself a good writer or an actor. I consider myself Liz Amplified Online. If I were to sit and think about things, nothing would get done.

Dave Do you think that because you can make a TikTok on your phone in seconds, there's something accessible about that that makes it a better tool for creative people?

Liz Part of the charm of the app is that accessibility. Anyone can pick up their phone. They have editing tools in the app for people to use. We all can consume it and that is attractive because there's no gatekeeping that way. On TikTok, you don't need any professional software or expensive cameras. It's just you and your phone and a couple of laughs.

Dave Walk me through the creation of your favorite TikTok.

Liz This is so silly, but it's the ones with my dad. I mean, he means the world to me. But it's just us riffing off each other, which I think is also the epitome of the app. I just placed the camera in front of him and he's like, "We're doing this again?" There's no plan and there's literally nothing special about it. His office has the worst lighting in the world. It's a horrible angle for both of us. I'm usually wearing no makeup and sweats and he's just double-chin in the chair. It's the best collab.

Dave What's your advice for people who want to create videos on TikTok?

Liz I have two pieces of advice. One, whatever you're creating, some things will be better than others and that's OK. That's part of the process. Don't be too hard on yourself because then you're stunting your own growth. My second piece of advice is that you will never make everyone happy, and that's great.

Dave Could you come up with your own prompt to open the chapter?

Liz I did one video where I walked outside with a microphone I'd just bought and commented on people's cars. It's just me being like, "That's a very nice car." I love corgis and two corgis walked by—I was so happy I screamed. And one person was texting and driving and I got mad. Go outside, record yourself talking about what you see.

Dave This is chapter one, so we'll be leading with, "Make sure to talk about your neighbor's corgis."

ORIGINAL TIKTOKS

It's easy to view TikTok as a place filled with only 15-second dance moves to popular new songs. You wouldn't be wrong. Technically, that is exactly the case for many TikTok users. However, the most creative and exciting moments on the app happen when someone posts a video with original audio. I once used the audio from a TikTok with a pig squealing. In my TikTok, the squealing was a fire alarm sound effect (it sounded just like a fire alarm, to be fair).

Making an original TikTok is the purest form of Internet. The key difference between these and an old YouTube video is that millions of people may use your audio and turn it into something entirely different.

#BookBeats

Open and close a heavy book to any beat you'd like. Perhaps Snoop Dogg's classic "Drop It Like It's Hot." You can even accompany the beat by singing along with the lyrics. The heavier the book, the better.

It doesn't hurt to pick a book with a peculiar title. Details like this are often are the secret sauce to going viral. The comment section may just fixate on your copy of *The Beekeeper's Bible* bopping along to an old rap song.

#BubbleWrapped

Walk on bubble wrap. Wear bubble wrap. Make a bubble wrap suit, if it pleases you. The key thing here is bubble wrap.

#MakeATikTokEveryDayReview

Give a book review. You don't have to be an expert. Just talk about a book you read. For example: "Hi everyone, today I'm going to talk to you about *Make a TikTok Every Day*. Wow! I was blown away from page one. The details, humor, and overall spirit of the book really got me into a creative mindset to make exciting, unique TikToks every day. Ten stars!"

#JustTheTwoOfUs

Create a sketch in which you are having a conversation as two or more people. This is a common approach to sketches on TikTok. Usually shot in a selfie mode, you film yourself having a back and forth conversation. You play every character. Often the characters are only differentiated by a t-shirt. Sometimes, it's just the text over their bodies, showing which character they're playing. A personal favorite: a towel over your head to represent long hair if you're playing a "mom" character.

This form has been perfected by @Lozclaws, who often posts full 60-second conversations. In one TikTok, she played several colleges in the U.S. and all the students. The trick with these TikToks is write a script beforehand that clearly provides a unique voice to each character. And, like so many successful videos, enthusiasm is really what sells.

#KitchenInstruments

Turn a regular household item into an instrument. Cups are now drums. A clothesline is a guitar string. A flickering candle lighter is now a metronome.

#ToiletTapDance

Tap dance on the toilet. Think this hasn't been done? It has.

#TikTokCarKaraoke

Record yourself singing to a song in the car.

#BadKaraoke

Sing a song! If you're great at singing, awesome. This is the platform for you. Thank me when one of the many record companies swarming TikTok signs you. If you're bad at singing, in some ways, this could be better.

Users love to take bad covers of songs and lay them over videos. Some of the best TikToks are poorly sung covers of old TV show theme songs. Those are typically 30 to 60 second songs and easy to identify within seconds, no matter how badly you sang the *Cheers* theme.

#BodyNotes

Create music using your body. Snap, clap, make that weird sound that happens when you blow a bubble with your cheek and flick it. There are endless possibilities. Resist flatulence, unless that's essential to your personal brand of humor.

#RoommateShowerSongs

From behind a closed door, record your friend singing to themselves in the shower.

#EveryAngle

Shoot a TikTok with several different camera angles. Liam Neeson's infamous fence jump in *Taken 3* was captured by no fewer than 13 camera angles. The whole shot is over within seven seconds, and it's the most unnecessary, wonderful sequence ever committed to film. Pay homage to it by shooting a mundane event from your life—making a cup of coffee, petting your dog—in the same way.

#WhyDidYouDoThat

Have a conversation with your conscience about a recent poor decision you made.

#TheLittleThings

Take a really close-up video of something. A caterpillar maybe. Or a dog's nose. Choose a song with the word "detail" in it.

#OnFire

Set something on fire. Do this safely, outside, preferably in a fire pit. If I learned anything in Boy Scouts, it's that setting stuff on fire and seeing how it burns is always interesting. Unless it has toxic chemicals (rest in pieces, football that instantly exploded).

#MyFirstDuet

Create a TikTok meant specifically for a duet. Users create duets on TikTok by filming themselves simultaneously with another TikTok. My favorite duet trend came from a video a user posted of her family reacting to her college admission letter. She got in and the family celebrated.

Very quickly, other users noticed something. The family was all facing the left side of the screen. Plus, the timing of the video allowed a small window for a dueter to briefly do something entirely underwhelming. As a result, thousands of TikTok users posted videos of themselves doing something mundane, such as eating a salad, to the delight of this extremely enthusiastic family.

Create something that will tempt others to duet with you, such as a one-sided conversation that allows people time to answer. In 2020, I did this as a quarantine waiter, taking orders from people who couldn't go out due to the pandemic.

The key to creating a duet-able TikTok is to interact with the left side of the screen in some way. High five. Karate kick. Lick the left side of the screen. Too weird? Fine, just high five. The main thing is to create an opportunity for collaboration.

 ### #MakeSomeMusic

Create original music or sound effects. It doesn't even have to make sense. Film yourself playfully hitting random piano keys and jumping around to each note.

 ### #ASMRtok

Go full ASMR (Autonomous Sensory Meridian Response). Put your phone next to some carrots and chop them with a sharp knife. The whole TikTok could just be chopping. I'm surprised more people don't devote entire channels to ASMR.

#AmbientWaterSounds

Film a body of water. A river, a waterfall, the ocean. Can you imagine scrolling through your TikTok feed and suddenly coming across a babbling brook? It would be strange if you didn't stop and watch this brook for a minute, then watch it again. It may be worth getting a microphone extension for your phone to really capture that delightful bubbly sound.

#PlantPepTalk

Say nice things to a house plant and see if it grows faster.

#PlantTrashTalk

Say mean things to a house plant and see if it dies.

#MyPlantBaby

Record a house plant growing over several weeks and edit the clips together to make a montage.

#CardboardChallenge

Make a TikTok that's one long take of you just trying to flatten a cardboard box before putting it in the recycle bin.

#LaughTrack

Create an over-the-top sitcom TikTok with a laugh track.

This may require the ability to edit. But if you don't have that, recruit your own studio audience! Get your whole family to laugh way too hard at every joke and interaction.

The easiest from of this is to have someone "come home." Basically, just open the door of your house, apartment, TikTok collab house, whatever, and give a friendly wave. For extra effect, say something overly corny. It's sure to get laughs from your '90s studio audience and a quiet chuckle from someone scrolling through TikTok.

#MusicMash

TikTok allows creators to create song mixes. So, mash two popular songs together, upload the video and see if anyone uses the audio. People often use "Frankenstein-ed" song lyrics in the funniest way imaginable.

#PlasticBagArt

Using the in-app voice-over feature on TikTok, you can record your own voice droning on with a melodramatic monologue. Record a plastic bag flying in the wind. Great, fun, weird original idea, right? Wrong, this is an unintentionally funny scene from *American Beauty*.

Never be afraid to reference a movie on TikTok, even if you fear no one will get the reference. If your reference is spot-on, it won't matter. After posting a *Groundhog Day* TikTok, I was told a few weeks later that someone's kid just "saw a movie based on that TikTok." In other words, funny is funny.

#BoardGameOver

Set up an entire board game. Use a game with a lot of pieces, like chess. The more pieces, the better. Set all the pieces up, press record on your phone, then upend the board and let the pieces fly.

It's a bit of a trope, throwing a board game. But how often do you really get to do it? Now you can let your emotions get the best of you without any consequences. Try to get it in one take.

#AdoptAStuffedAnimal

Act like you've adopted a dog and are raising it on TikTok. But it's really just a stuffed animal.

#BulbSmash

Crush old light bulbs (safely). Make sure to recycle them.

#AnimalNoise

Record an animal making a strange noise. Animal noises have endless potential for people to use as audio. And sometimes it's just interesting to hear a new animal sound!

#GreenScreenNews

Take a screenshot of a news story, use the "green screen effect" on TikTok, and explain the story with the screenshot behind you.

#TakeMyAdvice

Advice TikToks often feature creators speaking to the camera with genuine empathy and kindness. Speaking candidly from experience on TikTok can be refreshing for both creator and viewer. Best of all, no one can call it unsolicited advice. One can simply scroll right on past if it doesn't apply to them. Take my advice, this could work.

#DearDiary

Record a video diary. User @queen.spaghetti filmed herself moving to Alaska. Her ongoing TikTok entries were honest, self-effacing, funny, and inspiring. Allowing yourself to be vulnerable on video is not an easy task, but it can be rewarding.

The 60-second time limit on TikTok forces you to boil down your diary entry to the essentials. This can make you a better storyteller and allows for each TikTok to deal with a specific topic. Talk about your day, talk about a new project, talk about nothing. The TikTok algorithm will quickly let you know what appeals to people the most.

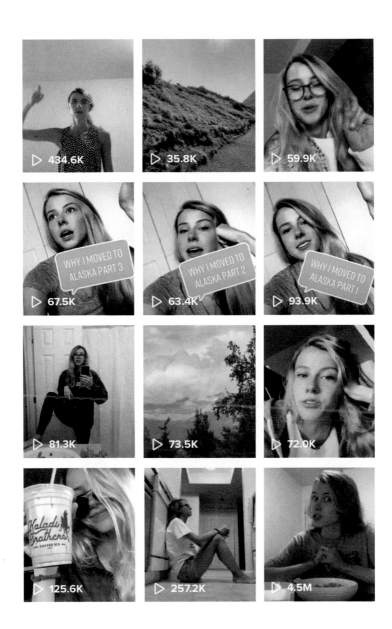

MUSIC, DANCING & LIP SYNCING TIKTOKS

INTERVIEW WITH

CIAN DUCROT
(@cianducrot)

Dave What is it about TikTok that you like so much?

Cian It's the most chill, laid-back, diverse platform. It's a very easy place to create content. It's also the least time consuming. When I did YouTube, it took me all day to make a video. On TikTok, I can make ten videos and people get so much more from them. You can interact on a more personal and instant level.

Dave How did you use social media before TikTok?

Cian I started making content for social media when I was 13. That was on Facebook and YouTube. I was posting covers, blogs and YouTube videos, and just anything I wanted to make. I continued to do that for as long as I could keep it up. I was also learning how to produce, put records out, and balance university. I just kept on going until I found things that worked and got better at it. And then it just blew up suddenly.

"I wanted to create a really personal place and to grow it in a way that people feel attached to me and my music and the world that I'm creating."

Dave Did you have that moment of checking your phone and saying, "Oh, my God, what's happening here?"

Cian Yeah, it was a little remix of a few songs. And then I put those together. It was a small blowup. It used to get 200, 300 views. And then I got around 20,000. I was like, "Oooh!" And then when I moved here, I started making videos with my roommates. That was millions of views. It was insane.

Dave Do you have any personal goals, short-term or long-term?

Cian One of my goals is to livestream every Sunday. I really want to do a livestream every Sunday. I'm gonna do it on this sofa here, like a talk show.

Dave You have five official music tracks on TikTok. What's it been like seeing your music on TikTok?

Cian I think I try to just feel the same as before. Although so much has changed in my life, I still try to keep the mindset that nobody's using my music or things aren't changing. Sometimes I look into it and I go, "That is so crazy! Random people in the world that I don't know are singing my lyrics." Obviously, I want to connect with my fan base, but not get so engulfed in this whole thing that I can't get my head out of it.

Dave When you make a TikTok, what's the response you're hoping to get?

Cian I just want people to enjoy it. I love reading the comments and seeing people's feedback. It's really nice to see that people can relate to the things that I say or the music that I make.

Dave You seem sort of unique in that way. You're more focused on the community than adding followers.

Cian Yeah, I think if I had been more interested in just the number of followers, I would have done something very different. I would have continued with the same videos that I know get millions of views. But I didn't want to just do that all over again. I wanted to create a really personal place and to grow it in a way that people really feel attached to me and my music and the world that I'm creating.

Dave I'm hoping to lead into the prompts with an idea from you.

Cian I'm gonna tell you two. Find a unique situation that you are in and talk about it. I was an Irish guy in America. That was a unique situation for me. And then when I moved in with the girls, I was a guy living with two girls. So I took those situations and gave my story about them. Another thing I love doing is going through comments of song requests, and using the reply feature and making a reply to somebody's comment. This makes it super personal to that person and also everybody that's watching, who are like, "Oh my God, maybe if I comment, you will reply!"

MUSIC, DANCING & LIP SYNCING TIKTOKS

Music is crucial to TikTok. It's why the app came into existence. TikTok started as Musical.ly, an app designed for lip syncing to popular songs. This is still a part of TikTok's DNA, but like all social media apps, and most things with DNA, it evolved into something bigger and better.

As much as the Boomers of the world may gawk at the Zoomers racking up millions of views on 15-second dance moves, the Charli D'Amelio's have the last laugh with their increasing popularity, endorsement deals, and well-earned place in modern pop culture.

So, keep up, watch me, and pay attention to these dance moves and original song ideas, because I'm only going to write these prompts once.

 ### #CharliWannabe

Find the most recent Charli D'Amelio dance and try it. It's not as easy as you think.

 ### #SameSongNewMeaning

Pick a popular song and backwards engineer the lyrics into a funny TikTok you can lip sync to. For example, I once decided I wanted to use the lyrics to the "See You Again" by Wiz Khalifa.

I also had in my head that I wanted to make a TikTok about Watergate, the 1970s scandal that eventually led to President Nixon's resignation.

We set up a scene in a parking garage in which a White House informant (played by my colleague Ron Charles) provides information to *Washington Post* reporter Bob Woodward, (played by me). I mouthed one line of the song, and in response, the informant lip synced the next line.

By taking the song "See You Again" and mashing them with a dramatic, serious scene based on the Watergate scandal, we made a classic lip sync TikTok from scratch.

35 #PianoRevisited

Play a song on the piano. That song you learned for the piano recital in fifth grade might be just the song someone wants to use as an audio for their TikTok. Maybe a complete stranger with 5 million followers will use it. You never know.

36 #LiteralInterpretation

Pick another song and reenact the lyrics literally, while lip syncing. For example, "We Didn't Start the Fire." Stand near a fireplace, reciting the chorus to this song while a fire roars in the background.

37 #NeverTooLateToRenegade

Learn the Renegade. Because it is one of the biggest viral dances ever, I'm fairly certain I am required by law to include this in a TikTok book.

#PoetsCorner

38

Write a poem and recite it in a TikTok. Poetry isn't dead on TikTok and there's a whole community waiting to hear your poem, good or bad or open to interpretation. Go full Beatnik and accompany your poem with a pair of bongos.

#MirrorChallenge

39

Pull off the #mirrorchallenge. This helps if you have a twin, but it's really about imitation and how well you know someone (and how well they know you).

Facing your twin or person-that-sort-of–looks-like-you, move in sync with them. Lip sync a song as you're imitating your partner. The intention is to make it seem as if you're looking in an actual mirror, but it's really just a person opposite you mirroring your every move.

This is a TikTok challenge that seems easy on the surface but can take hours to get right.

#MirrorJump

Film yourself dancing in the mirror, but include a few "mirror jumps." These are a fun, effective addition to any TikTok. Unlike the mirror challenge, this looks harder than it actually is. With your camera pointed at the mirror, jump up, then stop recording. Change outfits then jump again, starting to record as you land. This will create a truly dazzling effect that makes it seem as if you're jumping and transforming through mirror portals. But really, you're just goofing around in your bathroom.

#Choreographed

Pull off a dance move with choreography and several camera angles. Dance the first part of the newest TikTok song, then turn to your right. Stop shooting the TikTok, then begin shooting the TikTok from the new angle, executing the second part of the dance. Go on and on until the dance move is over. You're on your way to being a music video director!

#DanceBattle

Use the duet feature to dance side-by-side with a popular TikTok creator. This is a great way to really see just how well you've learned a dance. With the side-by-side aspect of duets, there's no escaping a wrong move. If you nail it, you'll very likely get some recognition for it. Duets with popular creators can get a boost, especially if the original TikToker you duetted likes or comments on the TikTok.

#OneSidedDanceBattle

Use the duet feature to dance side-by-side with a popular TikTok creator. This time, DON'T learn the dance. Try not to even watch the dance beforehand. Just see what happens on your first attempt. This is a lazy, but hilarious way to go viral. It's my personal favorite kind of dancing—the no effort kind.

#SlowDancePupper

Slow dance with your pet dog. People love dogs. You can't go wrong here.

#IKnowThisSong

Attempt to sing a song from memory. This will very likely go poorly, which in turn could create a wonderful audio, filled with funny mistakes and misquoted lyrics. A huge number of people still think Taylor Swift was saying "Starbucks lovers" instead of "list of ex-lovers" in her song "Blank Space." Why not reinforce that mistaken belief by singing it with those lyrics in your TikTok?

#LearningAnInstrument

Make a mini-documentary of yourself learning an instrument. This isn't a new idea, but it's always inspirational when someone tracks their progress on an instrument. Let's say you choose the trumpet. The first part of the TikTok is five seconds of you puffing out random notes. The next five seconds is after you've practiced for two weeks. Now it sounds like music at least. By the end of the TikTok, you're now playing "Flight of the Bumblebee" while hopping around on one foot.

Ok, that might be ambitious. But showing off even a little progress on a musical instrument is really inspiring. TikTok fosters positivity and encouragement. You might be surprised by the support you find.

#TikToksGotTalent

Write an original song. Upload it to the TikTok library. Become a star faster than anyone ever did on a TV talent show.

#GlassMusic

Tune glasses to several different notes by filling them with different amounts of water. You can do this by downloading a tuner app on your phone to help you get each one just right.

Make a whole show of it. Put on a tux or dress or something fancy. Line the tuned glasses up in front of you, pull out some spoons, and make beautiful music. It doesn't have to be good; but if it sounds vaguely like a song people know, that's a bonus.

 ## #DirtyDancingAgain

Re-create a famous music video or musical dance sequence shot for shot. *Dirty Dancing* is a start, or a particularly passionate '80s dance music video (arguably, the best kind of music videos).

If you can, put on the same outfit. Style your hair the same way. The closer you can resemble a memorable dance scene, the better. TikTok users will immediately recognize it and appreciate the attention to detail.

 ## #WeddingPlaylist

Make a playlist of "Songs that make people go crazy at weddings." Have the song change every five seconds and react with increasingly chaotic excitement.

 ## #PodcastBop

Dance to a popular podcast intro that happens to be a bop (shout out to the Post Reports podcast).

 ## #CommercialAcousticRadio

Perform an a cappella version of a popular commercial jingle.

 ## #StrangerDanceOff

Challenge a stranger to a dance-off. This could go horribly wrong. Be prepared to walk away if the person is not interested in being filmed or dancing. However, this could go very well and you may end up with a pretty impressive TikTok dance-off in the middle of a street with a stranger. Make sure to get the stranger's permission before uploading the video.

#OldSchoolMoves

Learn an old dance move from a few decades ago that no one on TikToks knows. Once you've mastered it, post a TikTok of the dance. Afterward, create a longer TikTok that is a tutorial of this dance. Walk the user through each dance move, repeating it slowly. Dance tutorials are huge on TikTok and rack up thousands of views and grateful comments.

 #MariachiLive

Record a live mariachi band. Interact with the band by requesting songs and asking their names.

 #MyMashup

Create a mashup of two popular songs using a sound application. Show the sound waves and the two clips as they come together to make a cohesive, catchy song.

 #SongRequest

Point your phone at some one you know that can sing well and request a song. Count down from four seconds and see what happens. If they can't sing well, that's fine too—and funny.

 #DrumrollPlease

Practice a drum roll. Record your process over several weeks and months until you can drumroll perfectly.

#FreeDance

Dance like nobody's watching, except your phone camera, which will be recording.

#TalkingWithMyHands

Find a very fast-paced song and point in the air at each beat.
Use the text-on-screen editor to add text each time you point.

#ParentsCanDanceToo

Dance with your parents. It's always adorable.

INTERVIEW WITH

MELISSA ONG
(@chunkysdead)

Dave So when did you first hear about TikTok?

Melissa I kind of vaguely knew what Musical.ly was because I had seen clips of it on Instagram. I converted when my best friend Brittany said, "You have to get TikTok." The first videos I was shown, I was just dying laughing.

Dave How did you get started?

Melissa I was posting one to two times a day, just trying to get the hang of it. And then I saw this guy who was posting a million times a day and growing really quickly. I was like, what if I just post a million times a day?

Dave You've always said quantity over quality. My understanding is that posting a ton doesn't actually hurt your account.

Melissa I have a contact at TikTok who I asked about the algorithm. I was like, "Is there any penalty to posting really frequently?" She was just like, "No." So I can just test all my ideas.

Dave Has there been a TikTok that you were surprised took off?

Melissa My first video to hit a million views was this one where I was like, "Teachers before they write on the board: I'm not an artist. Just bear with me." That hit a million views. I was like, wow, that's so exciting. And why? That wasn't a trend. That was just me being being weird.

"Whenever an idea pops into my head, which is a million times a day, I write it down and I just try and create it as quickly as possible."

Dave How would you define Alt TikTok?

Melissa It feels very raw and authentic. It's not the popular kids' TikTok. A lot of times it's low-quality video. I think people appreciate how random and serendipitous those videos are, because I think on TikTok, you're just scrolling through and trying to laugh.

Dave I want to know a little more about your process of making a TikTok.

Melissa Whenever an idea pops into my head, which is a million times a day, I write it down and I just try and create it as quickly as possible. I get inspiration by scrolling TikTok. I also draw inspiration from my real-life experiences. I don't like to put a lot of effort into my videos. Some people will be like, "Oh, I want this background, I'll go to this place." And I'm like, "No, I'm going to green screen an iStock photo in 280p for my background, because TikTok doesn't care about highly produced stuff."

Dave Do you think TikTok directly reflects Gen Z?

Melissa Absolutely. TikTok is so reflective of Gen Z and Gen Z humor. [The world] is so fast and changing and people are just more open to authenticity and weirdness.

Dave Where do you see TikTok in the next few years?

Melissa I think that just like anything else, it'll become more mainstream. Before it was just us and now celebrities are hopping on it. Charli D'Amelio is just as famous as Scarlett Johansson. So much of the attention now is on social media. Who even watches TV anymore, you know what I mean?

Dave Is that the new form of celebrity?

Melissa I think that it's very possible for social media stars to become more traditional celebrities. The unique leverage that social media stars already have is that they already have established a fan base.

ALT TIKTOKS

This area of TikTok is impossible to define partially because that's the whole point. When TikTok chose to highlight the #AltTikTok hashtag on their Discover page, in lieu of a standard brief description, they simply wrote, "Welcome to Alt TikTok."

Perhaps the easiest definition to apply to Alt TikTok is that it's not mainstream; it is, in fact, very strange. Many of these prompts are inspired by the evil geniuses that make up Alt TikTok, Melissa Ong included.

Ok, let's get weird.

#Frogging

For some reason, frogs are synonymous with Alt TikTok. So, find yourself a frog in a pond and film them. Make sure they're relaxing, then find a laid-back song to play behind your video. I suggest "We Fly High" by Jim Jones.

#OutdoorMonsters

Use the color correction effect to take video of animals outdoors. Frogs are an Alt TikTok favorite, but don't feel limited to amphibian creatures. Set it to some strange music.

#MiPanYouPanWeAllPan

The "Mi Pan Su Sus" audio is a favorite of Alt TikTok. The tune was originally a jingle for a Russian cereal, and later emerged on Alt TikTok in a video of an animated dancing llama, eerily coated in red light.

Challenge yourself to create an animation and set it to whatever interesting audio you can find . If your animation is awful (like all of my animations), that's even better! In the strange world of Alt TikTok, bizarre animation is a plus.

#BlankStare

Stare into the camera for sixty seconds without blinking.

#OneJoke

Pretend you're a stand-up comedian who only knows one joke. Tell it over and over again in multiple TikToks.

#FaceHandFriend

Draw a face on your hand and talk to it. Create an entire personality around this Face Hand. My version of this is a Spam can named Sam—the "P" is scribbled out so it reads "Sam".

Your Face Hand character should have a backstory, current motive, and a long future on your account. Maybe, in the end, your independent Face Hand will decide to move away, only to learn it's still attached to your body. When Face Hand is angry, argue with it. A 15-second TikTok in which a human argues with their own hand is peak Alt TikTok.

Your new friend could have existential crisis. Is he or she alone? Why doesn't the other hand have a face? Why do any of us have a face? As you can see, creating a character from a drawn-on face can generate content for an entire TikTok account. At the very least, you'll have someone to talk to.

#RecorderCover

Search "[your desired song] recorder cover" on YouTube, and you are almost certain to find a recorder cover. This surprising Internet truth was delivered to me by my friend and colleague, Teddy Amenbar, who told me that there is literally a recorder cover for every song. I laughed. That can't be true, right?

So far, I have found a recorder cover for every song I've ever searched on YouTube. Find your recorder cover of choice and use it in a TikTok.

#RealLifeBloopers

Post a montage of "bloopers" from your everyday life. Oops, you spilled coffee. Oh no, you forgot to go to a meeting. Darn, you didn't pay rent. End blooper reel.

#NauticalNonsense

Search "Spongebob" on TikTok and click through to audio.
You'll quickly find remixes people have created from the show.
Let one of these nautical audios inspire you. Dress up as one of
the many background fish, for instance. Use the green screen
effect to place yourself in the Krusty Krab. You can sit down
and have a burger while some weird Spongebob audio that a
14-year-old kid from New Zealand uploaded plays happily in
the background.

#SummerFun

Upload a montage of your "summer trip" but only show
pictures of yourself in your apartment. Play music specific to a
region that you do not live in.

#LavaDestroyedMyFamily

Green screen fabric is only around 20 to 30 bucks. Buy a green
screen blanket and go absolutely wild with it. Lay it down on
the ground and pretend it is actual lava. Use editing software
like Premiere Pro, Adobe After Affects, or Final Cut Pro to
replace the green screen with lava.

#WeatherReport

Use green screen fabric to give the weather forecast. Point at
parts of the screen and declare snowstorms in July.

#WhereAmI

Wrap yourself in green screen fabric and pretend it's an
invisibility cloak. This is easy to achieve if your camera stays in
one place. Simply stand there with the green screen wrapped
around you, then while still recording, walk away from the shot.
When editing, replace the green screen with the empty shot.
Now, it will look like your body truly disappeared.

75 #HomemadeCostume

Create a costume out of only the items in your house. A TikTok user called @theamazonbox created a costume out of Amazon boxes. That's the entire premise for the account. Every TikTok is a mischievous Amazon box monster with human arms and legs and an Amazon smile logo for a face. It's the best, strangest, most terrible creation to come out of TikTok and I encourage any aspiring TikTok-er to be that weird.

76 #TourismAd

Create a fake tourism video for your hometown. List "Ten things to do in [your city]." Make up odd things no one would ever do, or poke fun at things people actually do. For instance, if I made this video for Washington, DC, I might say, "Go to our museums," but it's just me staring at a blank wall.

#WineExpert

Pretend to be a wine tasting expert but don't share any real knowledge or demonstrate any understanding of what wine should taste like:

"I taste extra grape in this one."

#GroupTextKaraoke

In a group text, record a voice note of yourself singing the beginning of a song. Ask your friends to continue the song in voice notes. Download an app that allows you to record your phone's screen. Record as you scroll through the group text playing each voice note to make a complete song for your group text karaoke TikTok.

#NewBoardGame

Create an imagined board game. Draw a nonsensical board and add pieces from other board games. Gather friends and family around the fake board game and shoot a dramatic scene. It could be the moment someone's piece makes it to the center of the board and defeats the evil wizard.

Take it further and create real rules for it, and patent and sell the game when the TikTok goes viral. Write a book about your success and thank me in the acknowledgments.

#TechnoCrossStitch

Learn to cross-stitch. After you've acquired this skill, take a time-lapse video of yourself cross-stitching something. Set it to techno music.

#MyChickenSon

Pretend to hatch an egg. Take care of the egg in a montage until it cracks open and becomes a chicken. Refer the chicken as your child.

82

#YouHaveEntered

Create a "You have entered ___ Alt TikTok" TikTok. All this meme requires is a commitment to a theme. For example, if you bake, your TikTok is you dancing with a rolling pin. The text on screen reads, "You have entered baking Alt TikTok." Pair this video with the audio that always accompanies this meme, and congratulations, you've created a new Alt TikTok.

#MyInnerThoughts

Show what the conversations in your own head are like. Write down your inner dialogue as it's happening, then actually shoot it. You can easily re-create this in selfie mode, alternating between two angles of yourself.

#ReplyAll

Often, people will comment on TikToks with something that doesn't make sense, or a question that the creator really can't answer. "Why did you wear that?" they'll ask, or "Who are you, why are you on my For You Page?"

Exact your revenge using the comment reply function. Reply to them in video form, but don't actually address their question. It's dumb, but that's kind of this whole chapter.

#FoundFootage

Shoot a found-footage-style TikTok. The movie *The Blair Witch Project* popularized this creepy style of storytelling, where the audience sees the events through the characters' cameras. Your TikTok could involve the subject filming something scary at night, dropping their phone, and running away. As the phone lays on the ground at the end, something appears in the shot. It could be something mundane, like a picture of your tax returns, or something scary like a creepy old doll. Either way, this is a fun way to play with suspense.

#WhatsInMyNose

Pick your nose but when you pick it, cut to a close up to reveal you picked something completely impossible out of your nose.

#RoombaBets

Make a grid on your floor with tape and cover it in dirt. Have one or more roombas roam around for a minute. Take bets on which square gets cleanest.

#SuperFan

Claim you are now a super fan of an obscure sports team. Devote weeks to TikToks about that team. For instance, a friend and I once became very attached to the Charlotte Checkers Hockey team—a team we have never seen play in person or on TV. I still cherish my Charlotte Checkers t-shirt.

89 ## #HotDogDogEatingContest

Hold a hot dog eating contest between you and your dog.

90 ## #TurnOffTheLights

Do a TikTok in the dark. Have someone flip the lights on for just half a second in your 10- to 15-second Tiktok. Be in a strange or compromising position in that half second.

#BackInTheBottle

Record yourself drinking an entire half gallon of milk, then reverse the footage and post it.

92 ## #TableOfContents

Find an old, large, dusty book that no one is using. Glue the pages together, then cut a secret hole in the book, page by page, using a trapezoidal blade. Once you've created a hiding place in the book, hide something completely ridiculous in the book. Make a TikTok revealing this hidden item.

93 ## #StuffedHuman

Pretend you are filling with stuffing like a stuffed animal. Illustrate this by showing stuffing coming out of your button-up shirt. Add another character who enters the room as you panic and try to put your stuffing back in.

INTERVIEW WITH
CORY BRADFORD
(@thisiscory)

Dave How do you come up with your History TikToks?

Cory I've been a history buff for a really long time. So a lot of it is general knowledge, and some specific details I just throw in there. I take those key bullet points and turn them into "movie lines." I'm just creating dialogue out of the situation, like if you were in the room with these historical figures, but I modernize the language. It makes it more relatable.

Dave Where are you editing your TikToks?

Cory I edit on my laptop. I've got a film school background, so the editing process is usually just importing it onto my computer and editing it there.

Dave You mentioned film school—tell me more about your background.

> "A lot of high school students started following me, saying, 'Hey, I'm passing quizzes because of these videos.'"

Cory I tried to do the traditional four year university. It just didn't fit for me. So I ended up going to art school for about two and a half years. I got my associate's in film and then later went back to school and eventually got a bachelor's in communications. Over the years I've tried to do different little videos on YouTube and Instagram. Nothing really caught on. It was my brother who kept telling me, check out this app, TikTok. It was a little weird at first, but then I started seeing a lot of young people doing comedy skits and stuff like that. And I've also done stand up before. I just started making little one-minute skits. One day I was like, "I'll do something about World War II, I'm a history buff." I did that and it blew up.

So I thought, "I guess I might as well do World War I now." I started doing different things in history. A lot of high school students started following me, saying, "Hey, I'm passing quizzes because of these videos."

Dave You have CEO of History on your bio. Is there a particular aspect of history that you enjoy covering most on a TikTok?

Cory A lot of it is US history, just different eras of it. I've done a couple of English monarchies, but I've always been really big on US history.

Dave I think recently there's this desire, especially among Americans, for us to get history right. What you and I were told about Christopher Columbus in school is probably very different from what they're being told now. Are there any takeaways you want your audience to have?

Cory I want people to form their own opinion. But on the other hand, for instance, I did a couple of videos where I showed the lead-up to the Civil War. Different things like the Missouri Compromise and Compromise of 1850. I just wanted people to see, it's kind of ridiculous that we even had a Civil War. This didn't have to happen. I do want people to kind of look at certain things and draw parallels to what's going on now in America and say, well, maybe we should do things a little differently so we can avoid some of the mistakes of the past.

Dave I think you mentioned in a caption in one of your videos, "Hey, this isn't my real job, by the way." What is your real job?

Cory I do campaign work. I've done it off and on for the last three years for a variety of political campaigns. But in my political history videos, I want people from all sides to be able to laugh at themselves and be entertained by it.

Dave I definitely think you accomplish that. I watched the one where you described every political party and what they had to offer.

Cory (laughs) Yeah and politically speaking, myself, I'm independent. I work for different campaigns, but they're usually moderate campaigns. I'm not really too far into one side or the other. So it's easy for me to make light of how serious all of this is being taken. But having a political background, I can see these things for what they are rather than what they want us to see them for. It makes it easier to play with the satire.

HISTORY TIKTOKS

A century from now, or honestly even a week from now, historians will be looking back at the early years of TikTok with great interest, trying to figure out how it came to be. What happened? Why? Was this a cultural moment that a random lip sync app just happened to reflect? My only hope is they get to History TikTok first.

A huge, diverse community of historians and history lovers publish thousands of History TikToks a day, educating an audience that is surprisingly receptive to history on an app most widely known for 15-second dances and memes.

#TheHistoryOfTikTok

Make a TikTok explaining the history of the app.

#WeDidntStartTheSequel

Search "We Didn't Start the Fire Karaoke version" and use that audio to tell the history of a time period or movement. Fit as many events, people, and places into the song as you can. Make sure to end with "WE DIDN'T START THE FIRE!"

#HistoricalInaccuracies

A significant portion of History TikTok takes the time to correct historical inaccuracies and common misconceptions. Creators may choose to highlight a woman who has traditionally been overlooked in favor of male figures in history. This can be done with music or significant lyrics in the background but it's often equally effective when the TikTok user is just speaking straight to camera as photos of the figure populate the screen.

#ShortDoc

Create a short documentary telling the story of a significant or totally insignificant historical moment. Record "talking heads"—people who specialize in the subject talking straight to camera. If you choose a serious topic, make sure it can be explained in 60 seconds. Include photos or video of the event. Or you could take a silly route, creating a mockumentary about an embarrassing childhood event. "Dave's first kiss," for instance, would include confessionals from several high school friends, detailing the weird events that led to the moment, and the instant messages exchanged later that night. The more serious the tone, the funnier it will be.

#TimeTravelHistory

The electro-swing remix of the song *"I Wanna be Like You"* from *The Jungle Book*, is often used to signify time travel on TikTok (I don't know why, don't ask me). Create an educational version of this meme to teach a moment in history.

In this meme, the time traveler appears out of thin air. This quick trick is done by shooting an empty space for half a second and then recording again as the "time traveler" jumps into the room.

Consider what time period the time traveler is coming from. A time traveler from the past may be surprised to discover everyone has a library of information in their pockets but just uses it to make TikToks.

#FullCongress

Introduce historical figures as if they are characters in a retro sitcom. With text on screen, have each figure turn to the camera and pose, in the style of the *Full House* opening credits. For example, a sitcom called *America's Founding Fathers* might show Benjamin Franklin, Thomas Jefferson, George Washington, John Adams, and Alexander Hamilton turning to the camera in various outfits and poses. *First Wave Feminists* would feature Sojourner Truth, Jane Addams, and Dorothy Day turning boldly to the camera. The more elaborate the costumes, props, and poses, the better.

 #UnimportantHistory

Explain the history of an object that seems unimportant. Spam, for instance, originated toward the end of the Great Depression as a long-lasting meat that didn't need to be refrigerated. It quickly gained popularity in World War II as a go-to food for the U.S. military. Today, it's sold in stores across the U.S. and is especially popular in Hawaii. This TikTok could show the different target demographics for Spam over the last 80 years, using different outfits and settings but with the same can of Spam (the design is almost completely unchanged).

 #GrandmasStory

Record your grandparents or parents talking about a childhood memory.

 #HistoricalAnecdote

Tell a historical anecdote—anything that can be covered in less than 20 seconds. For instance, I once discovered a story of how a young Julius Caeser was captured by pirates. You could simply describe the event straight to camera, or you could act it out as a sketch. Really boost your history-telling game by multiplying yourself into, for example, a crowd of pirates, using the crowd group effect.

#HistoryDontLie

Use the flute cover of Shakira's "Hips Don't Lie" in a TikTok. This pleasantly odd audio is a popular choice for TikToks about Medieval or Tudor history.

Locate this audio by searching the #MedievalTikTok hashtag, where you will find more than 40K users with large belts strapped over untucked, button-down white shirts playing a recorder that's been stored away in a box since fourth grade.

Take this audio and run with it. Creator @lucas_millership portrayed an entire back-and-forth conversation between Henry VIII and Anne Boleyn. With more than 300k likes, it's truly impressive to see such a dense, text-heavy post get so much attention on an app that many believe is just for dancing.

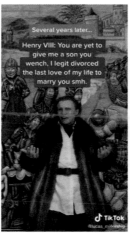

#DanceForHistory

Dance nonstop in the background as text appears on screen describing an historical event. This is the equivalent of a history teacher doing anything they can to get students to pay attention, and there's nothing wrong with that.

#ColonialHistory

Make a TikTok that explains historical events using modern language. Creator @thisiscory made an immensely popular TikTok about colonialism and World War II, in which various countries react to Germany claiming, "I want all this sh*t."

Taking historical events and distilling them into modern language can make these moments more accessible.

 106

#ThingsThatAnnoyHistoryBuffs

If you are a history expert or history major, make a TikTok about "Things That Annoy History Buffs."

 107

#FamousSpeechTakeTwo

Re-create a famous speech. For example, you could demonstrate the moment former President Theodore Roosevelt was shot in the chest while giving a speech. The speech tucked inside his jacket was so thick, it obstructed the bullet and saved his life. Moments in history like this that are visual and fairly brief are perfect fodder for TikTok.

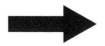

#SlideshowHistory

Download photos that illustrate a story in history and use the voice-over feature on TikTok to tell it over a slideshow. Many historians use the in-app slideshow effect and voice-over feature to great effect. And best of all, people learn something!

 #TheHistoryOfToday

Imagine yourself in twenty years attempting to explain current events to a future high school history class. For example, you may try to explain the Coronavirus pandemic:

Teacher: In the U.S., many citizens refused to wear masks.

Student: But teacher, wouldn't this infect and kill others?

Teacher: Yes, Johnny, they knew this. They just didn't care.

Student: That's messed up.

Teacher: Yeah.

 #HistoryOfReligion

Religious history can be a very engaging corner of TikTok. TikTok offers so many opportunities to educate others on religion and religious history. For example, many Muslim creators have made TikToks explaining the origins of Ramadan.

 #SameWordNewMeaning

Pick a word with a meaning that has changed over time. Explain what the word meant in the past. This could be a person lighting a candle in the past and saying, "It's lit," followed by a modern-day person at a party yelling, "IT'S LIT!"

 #WarTimeTalks

Create a TikTok about a war in history that was won through negotiations. Reimagine what the conversation would look like. Play the part of the many leaders involved.

#DaVinciModel

Choose a famous painting—*The Last Supper,* for instance.
Act as if you're the model posing for Leonardo da Vinci.

#BuildingBlocksOfHistory

Find an old building near to you and try to find out its history.
I recently learned my favorite Chinese food takeout place is in
the same building where John Wilkes Booth and his associates
planned Abraham Lincoln's assassination. Specifically, it was
planned in one of the karaoke rooms upstairs. History is wild!

#BriefMomentInTime

Take a deep breath and tell the entire history of a specific
event in one breath.

#TourThroughHistory

Visit a historic site and record the tour. Take all of your footage
and edit it into a 60-second-or-less highlight reel.

#BeforeItWasAPark

Go to a national park and take a video of a particularly pleasing
patch of nature. Narrate the video with the history of the area
and how it came to be a park.

#OldPSA

Find old black and white PSAs that are fair use. Pick out the
funniest clips and post them.

#BenFranklinInsta

Show what historical figures would say if they had social media.

#LAWNMOWERS

Look up the history of lawnmowers. Become an expert. Once you are a lawnmower scholar, rev up a lawnmower and yell the history of the useful grass cutters over the sound of the engine.

#OldPaperDocuments

Make a list of the oldest government legislation around the world. From most recent to oldest, record yourself using the "green screen" feature with each historical document behind you.

#OlympicHistory

Go on a run. When you're reaching the end, or are out of breath—whatever comes first—open your phone's selfie camera and record yourself telling the history of a historic Olympic event. Explain what happened and any historical or statistical significance. End the TikTok by stopping your run and saying a broken, breathless goodbye. Bestow a gold medal upon yourself for added effect. Bite into it. A gold wrapped chocolate gold medal would be ideal (and hilarious).

INTERVIEW WITH

JEFFERY DANG
(@jeffery.dang)

Dave How would you categorize your TikToks?

Jeffery My TikToks are mainly fashion. I actually started off doing Comedy TikToks, but I realized I wanted to make fashion content.

Dave Was it that you felt more passionate about fashion or you liked making Fashion TikToks more?

Jeffery Actually, I wanted to start a YouTube channel for fashion videos, but didn't. I thought, why not try TikTok instead?

Dave What was it about TikTok that made it more appealing?

Jeffery TikTok gives you a platform to post more. You can post three times a day, more if you want. Whatever comes to your mind, you can just post it right away. And especially because Vine is gone. I feel like that's why so many people enjoy TikTok, because it's such a Vine "energy" in a new platform.

"I made one video and it just kind of popped off from there."

Dave How did you first hear about TikTok?

Jeffery So you know those popular pages that just repost TikToks? I was like, "What is this platform? I thought I'll just hop on and see what it's about. And I'm like, I freaking love this."

Dave So what was your first TikTok that went viral?

Jeffery It was my TikTok where Mrs. Incredible trips, has a costume malfunction and her mask falls off.

The song "Murder on my Mind" by YNW Melly is playing in the background. It reached over 92 million views and 12.8 million likes.

Dave Walk me through your process.

Jeffery I'm also on the Chinese TikTok *[the Chinese version of the app, Douyin]*. With TikTok, there's so many genres but I feel like with the Chinese version, it's more catered to fashion content. So I'm on it every day to get inspiration.

Dave Is that window into Chinese fashion something your followers respond to?

Jeffery Definitely. If it wasn't for TikTok, Chinese fashion would not be trending. The process of downloading Chinese TikTok—changing your region, your address, and everything— I don't think anybody would do that just for fashion content. So, I was like, oh, maybe this would be a good thing to share. I made one video and it just popped off from there. I feel like Chinese fashion has had a direct influence on our fashion. American celebrities wear the most basic sweatwear. With Asian culture, they're putting on a full outfit. That's what I think is so cool. It's definitely influenced Gen Z and maybe early millennials to dress up.

Dave I feel like it's globalizing fashion a little more, too.

Jeffery Yeah, for sure. For example, in the U.K. and then in Asia, fashion would boom first and then the U.S. would get bits and pieces from it years later. Now that we have access to this type of content, everybody is on trend with fashion, across the globe.

Dave Can you give me an idea for a Fashion TikTok?

Jeffery A lot of creators have made a TikTok showing their cheapest and most expensive outfits. Most of the time the cheapest outfit is so much more stylish, and people love that.

HEALTH, FASHION & BEAUTY TIKTOKS

In today's world, and especially on TikTok, talking about mental health is much less taboo. Therapy is good! Toxic masculinity is bad! Gen Z, the first generation to grow up with a smart phone in their pockets, sees the Internet not as a fantasy, but a real place with real consequences.

And so, this chapter includes prompts on fashion and beauty, but also health. Some are goofy, some are more serious. Whatever the case, they are a reflection of a generation that prioritizes health differently.

 ### #FavFit

Make a montage of your favorite outfits. This might be a video or just photos of mirror selfies. Song choice is important, too!

 ### #OneStrutTenOutfits

Edit together a montage of yourself in different outfits but making the exact same movement.

Let's say the video is you walking up to the camera, showing off your outfit, then walking off the camera. Repeat this exactly in ten different outfits, then string the footage together into one cohesive and continuous act, with the outfits changing every couple of seconds.

 ### #ClothesFoldingForDummies

Make a TikTok on how to efficiently fold clothes, showing each individual step slowly. There are plenty of YouTube videos on how to do this.

In the TikTok, fold the clothes into a suitcase. When you're done, have someone else fold you and try to put you in the suitcase.

 ### #Acupunctured

Get acupuncture. Have a friend record it.

#HowToMakeup

Show off one of your makeup or beauty tips slowly without edits. Encourage followers to duet it in real time. Comment on the videos that duet and compliment them! Truly become the teacher in this setting by interacting with your "students."

#SunburnProblems

Make a TikTok about the importance of wearing sunscreen. Cover your face in orange peels and present yourself as the future version of yourself

Set the TikTok a few decades in the future: The text on-screen says, "The year 2051."

Kid: Papa, why is your face so leathery and wrinkled?

You: Because I never wore sunscreen, my child.

Kid: But it's so easy to do.

You: [looking directly to the camera.] I know. It really was.

#MorningRoutineOnLoop

Set up a camera or phone to record your morning routine. Start the TikTok by popping into the frame like you just splashed water on your face in the sink, out of sight. End the TikTok by ducking out in the same direction. Speed up the footage in the middle, so the video shows you getting ready in 15 seconds, to create an addictive loop.

#GrandpasClothes

Find some of your parents' or grandparents' old clothes and pick a song from the same era. Try on the clothes and dance around as if you're at a '70s disco, or whatever suits the clothes.

If you have a picture of your parents in the outfit, end the TikTok in the exact same pose, and cut to the picture.

#BackInStyle

Talk about an item of clothing that went out of style for everyone but you. The bootcut jean, for instance. Why is this item or style of clothing so important to you? Why is clothing significant to anyone? Answer those deep questions about clothes we all are desperate to understand. You never know, you might accidentally relaunch a fashion trend...

#AestheticLenses

Demonstrate how different certain styles of glasses or sunglasses can look depending on the shape of your face. Gather up a bunch of different frames or head to a glasses store. Make sure the camera and your head are in the exact same position as you try on different pairs. Then do the same thing with the same glasses but for someone else. Use a song with lyrics related to shapes and sizes.

#WaxedOff

Get your legs or chest waxed. Have a friend record that, too.

 #OuterVsInnerMe

Make a TikTok playing on the difference between your outer and inner self. Sometimes, being honest and self aware is essential to living a healthier life. Demonstrating your own inner struggles sometimes helps to deal with the day-to-day of being human.

Set up the TikTok with text over two versions of yourself: Outer Me and Inner Me.

Outer Me: Hey how are you! What a beautiful day!

Inner Me: I'm happy to see you but I really hope this interaction lasts less than 30 seconds.

Outer Me: Oh I'm doing great! Pretty normal day for me.

Inner Me: I just want to go home and sleep.

Outer Me: OK, talk to you later!

Inner Me: I have no idea when I will talk to you next and it's not high on my priorities.

It can be hard to do when you feel low, but reaching out and expressing your feelings can be really helpful.

 #MyStory

Talk frankly about a disease or condition that has affected you or someone in your family. This is a serious prompt, no doubt about that, but opening up about topics that might be considered taboo is healthy for everyone. TikTok has many tight-knit, thoughtful communities all dealing with similar struggles, ready to welcome in more TikTokers.

 #SuperFace

Attempt to paint your face into your favorite superhero. Even if it turns out poorly, surprise someone with your newly painted face and record their reaction.

#HelpMeDecide

Can't decide what to wear? Go live on TikTok and let your audience weigh in with their good fashion sense.

#Bedazzled

Customize an item of clothing. Stitch it up, bedazzle it, add pockets, do anything you want to it.

If you're happy with it, it could become your signature look.

#ShirtToKilt

Think outside the box and demonstrate how an everyday piece of clothing can be used in a different way. For example, a plaid shirt tied around your waist becomes a makeshift kilt. To complete the look, turn your vacuum upside down, hold it in your arms and pretend it's bagpipes. Vacuum afterward because you already got the vacuum out, so you might as well.

#BloodSavesLives

Go donate blood and encourage others to do so by recording your experience. Make sure to emphasize just how easy it is and that one person donating blood can save several lives.

#MyInsanePetPeeve

Describe what makes you irrationally angry, more so than most people. Is it a sound? A thing other people say? A particular person in your life? Demonstrate your reaction when that terrible thing happens to you. Narrate it with dramatic music.

Here's mine:

Dave is just sitting there minding his own business. The phone rings. The person on the other end begins talking—but wait— they are still eating! And worse, they're chewing directly into the phone. The noise is unbearable. My misophonia (which is very real!) causes me to cripple over in uncomfortable silence. I literally die. The TikTok ends with a short funeral. The person presiding over the funeral explains "he died of a person talking on the phone while chewing." Attendees at the funeral nod solemnly. This is, naturally, the worst way to die.

#IAmFashion

Attempt to create a new fashion trend—either one you're very passionate about or one you just made up. Generate a hashtag for it. See how many TikTok users you can get to follow this trend and use the hashtag.

Some ideas:

- ⊙ Suspenders and shorts #SuspenderShorts
- ⊙ Flip flops with formal wear #FormalFlips
- ⊙ Only buttoning the middle of a shirt #MiddleButtoning

#EightGlassesOfWater

Test out the old "drink eight glasses of water a day" advice. Record yourself every time you drink a glass of water and describe how it's making you feel. Talk about your level of hydration and really get over-the-top and overzealous in describing your love for water. At the eighth glass have a huge, monumental epiphany. You know the secret to life! And now you will share it... But the video cuts away. You ran out of time.

#MissingPiece

Complete a puzzle except for one piece of the puzzle. Use the text editor to put something on the big puzzle and text on the small piece.

The big puzzle could say "my life goals." Then, place the last piece of the puzzle. The text over this last piece says your biggest life goal. That might be world peace, a cute sleeping dog, or pizza. Anything! This could be sweet or funny.

#PostWorkoutGlow

Record yourself before and after a workout. The first half is before you get started, fresh-faced, ready to exercise. Then cut to the moment you finish the workout, out-of-breath, red-faced, sweaty, and tired.

You: Hey guys about to go on my run! Will check in when I'm done.

You: I'm done [labored breathing]. Thanks for [more heavy breathing] watching my [gasp] ... TikTok.

#AlwaysInStyle

Use the green screen effect to show off something that has "never gone out of style." This could be a trench coat, a plaid shirt, or jeans. Find photos from different eras and have them flash in the background while you show off your timeless style.

#TikTokCarpet

Watch a major red-carpet event and grab screenshots of various outfits. Act as a fashion critic and give your thoughts on each outfit. Or, dress up like you're a member of the press and imagine an interview with the celebrity, asking why they chose that outfit.

#WhatsInMyCoat

Find a long coat and see how many things you can put in it. Make a TikTok that's just you taking stuff out of the coat.

A list of things to put in your coat:

- ⭕ A board game
- ⭕ A stuffed animal
- ⭕ Candy
- ⭕ A baguette
- ⭕ This book
- ⭕ Another copy of this book
- ⭕ Encyclopedia Britannica
- ⭕ A gaming console
- ⭕ A rotary phone
- ⭕ Another jacket (then put that jacket on.)

#CryMeARiver

Wear an outfit entirely made out of denim. Strut to a Britney Spears or Justin Timberlake song (or maybe a Justin Timberlake song about Britney Spears). You could also persuade a friend to denim up and join you.

#HoodieZip

A perennial favorite on TikTok—put on a ton of zip-up hoodies at once and unzip them to the audio originated by user @normaflores52. It's the opening lines of the song "Stand by Me," which just happens to really sound like someone is unzipping a zipper.

This same audio was also used by users CHOPPING OFF THEIR OWN HAIR in real time. Personally, I don't recommend this but to each their own.

#JorgensonProgram

Parody unhealthy "wellness" culture by talking up a new lifestyle trend you just "discovered." Make up a name. A last name or place name is usually a good way to sell something.

You: I just started the Jorgenson Program. It's been amazing and I wanted to tell you all about it. *[Use all the generic tropes people talk about when describing a new health trend. Once you've totally sold this new lifestyle, take a dramatic pause, then say]* All you have to do is turn off TikTok once in a while and breathe oxygen outside.

#Spandexercise

Make an '80s-style workout video with your friends. Acquire neon, spandex outfits. They must be accessorized with multiple sweatbands and, ideally, also leg warmers. Stand in a group and make up ridiculous moves. None of them have to make sense at all. Pick an upbeat '80s song—there's certainly plenty of them to choose from.

#BringBackGloves

Try to make gloves popular. Not winter gloves, but silk gloves that people wear for formal occasions. Show how great they look, how versatile they are (they go with everything, right?), how useful they are. Stop at nothing to bring back silk gloves.

#RightTemperature

Record yourself checking your temperature to an appropriate song, such as "Temperature" by Sean Paul.

INTERVIEW WITH

MARIYUM CAKES
(@mxriyum)

Dave Your most successful TikTok is making an Oreo shake for your brother. It has a million likes. What was it like getting that reaction?

Mariyum Back then, I was just playing around. One night, my brother asked me to make him a shake and I'm like, why not make a TikTok out of this? I think I had 3,000 likes by the end of the night. When I woke up, it had 30K and it was just going up and up. It was a really cool moment. That's what started it for me. It gave me the encouragement that I needed.

Dave What did your TikTok look like beforehand?

Mariyum My TikTok before was sewing and painting, just random hobbies that I felt would be cute to post. But after that video, I tried to make it a little bit more cohesive. I wanted it to be a calming platform for people to enjoy and replay.

"I think TikTok is amazing because everybody kind of has short attention spans."

Dave That's what I like about your account. It fits a lot into 60 seconds, without being overwhelming.

Mariyum In my old videos, my voice is very sped up. Now when I do a voice-over, I go hide in a room and I do 50 takes.

Dave Is there a type of food that people like most?

Mariyum My fried chicken videos do really well. Fried chicken waffle sliders have been amazing. There's creativity behind them. Plus, it's fried chicken!

Dave Are you shooting all of them on a phone?

Mariyum It's all on my phone. I actually record on my Mom's spice rack. [laughs] I set up the spice rack and lay my phone on a towel. It's funny because everybody in the comments is like, "What kind of equipment do you use?"

Dave You're on Instagram as well and have a pretty decent following.

Mariyum Every platform serves a different purpose. I think TikTok is amazing because everybody kind of has short attention spans. My TikTok followers go to Instagram to read ingredients and measurements. People are also asking me to start a YouTube channel so the videos are a bit longer and more in-depth.

Dave How much of your food training is self-taught?

Mariyum I would say 50 to 60 percent of it. My mother was a chef, so I've also learned a lot from her, although food-wise, we're very different. My Dad also has a restaurant.

Dave Oh, wow. What are your parents' thoughts on your TikTok channel?

Mariyum In the beginning, they thought I was just playing around, which I was. Now I have more than 300,000 followers on TikTok. My Mom is so supportive and so excited. She sends me recipes. Now they're seeing how much effort I put into it, they're proud.

Dave That's so cool. What is your favorite TikTok that you've made?

Mariyum My favorite recipe so far was a Strawberry Stuffed Cheesecake French Toast. I wasn't expecting it to taste as amazing as it did.

Dave If someone wanted to make a Food TikTok, what would you suggest to them?

Mariyum Pasta does really well because it's so versatile. I think it's a good way to go, especially if you're starting out. Sandwich videos are also good. People like quick and easy recipes that also taste good and look good. You have to believe in your own creativity and how you want your videos to look. When you're creating food that you enjoy personally, the videos are always going to turn out better.

FOOD TIKTOKS

What separates Food TikTok from other food videos on the Internet is the encouraging environment, particularly for novices. We would all love to make delicious entrees and impress our friends with those entrees, but where do you even start? Creators on Food TikTok encourage beginners to "start today," not only with their inspiring videos, but also their warm captions and active comment sections.

So let's have some fun, because food should never not be fun.

#FirstAttempt

Record yourself making a brand-new recipe you've never even attempted before. Even if it goes poorly, splice the TikTok together and post it. You have to eat it too. No chickening out.

#SodaTasting

Perform an elaborate wine tasting, but for soda. Use terms like "crisp," "fruity," "full-bodied," etc. Pick a soda that comes in multiple flavors and varieties, and let people know your extremely detailed thoughts about each of them. Does it taste better from a plastic bottle or a can? How does the sugar-free version hold up against the original?

#FoodServiceHorrorStories

If you have experience in the food industry, record yourself talking about it. Mimic the most common questions customers ask waiters. A huge portion of TikTok has experience dealing with terrible customers and there can never be enough relatable TikToks about customer service.

Use text that will immediately draw someone in. For instance: "what it's like to be a waiter on Valentine's Day" or "when the customer leaves a terrible tip but hasn't left yet."

158 #GiantFood

Make a giant version of a food. You don't have to break a Guinness World Record (though it'd be cool if you did!), but making giant food is always funny. Giant pizza, giant cookie, giant whatever—make it happen!

159 #OneFoodSkill

Show how to do one specific skill, as opposed to an entire recipe. TikToks can only be sixty seconds max and some of us need help with the basics! For example, show how to peel a potato, crack an egg, or marinate meat.

#InnerWaiterDialogue

Make a voice-over of the inner dialogue of a waiter, barista, or other food server. Say something out loud in the TikTok, then pause while a voice-over says what you really think.

Waiter: Oh no, sir. That's not a problem. I can divide this into six checks.

Voice-over: WHY CAN'T ONE PERSON PAY AND YOU ALL COULD PAY THAT PERSON?

Waiter: Oh, please take as long as you need.

Voice-over: GET OUT OF HERE SO WE CAN CLOSE THE RESTAURANT AND LEAVE!

For many this will be a shared experience, but for those who've never worked in a restaurant it'll show them what's really going on. Win-win!

#OldFoodInTheBlender

Take all the old food in your house and throw it in a blender. I would not recommend that you also eat it!

#DonutChallenge

Perform the classic "try to eat a powdered sugar donut without licking your lips" challenge. Try this challenge solo, or compete with a friend. It's harder than you think!

#HowToMakeEggs

Show five (or more!) different ways to cook an egg. There's an especially hypnotizing video of chef Gordon Ramsay making scrambled eggs on TikTok that I've probably watched 50 times. He makes these perfect eggs and the entire time it's complete chaos. It's as if someone put a timed bomb on his back and said it would go off if he didn't make the scrambled eggs in under two minutes.

Bring that chaotic energy into this TikTok. Show all the different types of eggs in either one or several TikToks. Eggs are fairly universal, but so many people could be better at making eggs. Just eggsperiment.

#FaceCake

Order a "face cake" of yourself and eat it. For the uninitiated, a "face cake" is a cake with a photo of yourself on it. Technology finally peaked when we learned to print real, edible photos onto the top of cakes.

#WhichPizzaTopping

Make a TikTok asking your followers to comment with various pizza toppings. Reply to your favorite suggestion with a video showing the pizza. Video reply comments are a really effective way to interact with followers. And who knows, maybe this journey will lead you to unexpectedly enjoying an anchovy pizza. Not far enough? Go the distance and make a pizza with all the toppings from the comments.

#NewCuisine

Try your hand at a foreign cuisine totally out of your regular wheelhouse.

#TimeLapseBake

Turn on the time-lapse feature on your camera and record something slowly baking in the oven. Bread, or anything that rises, is ideal for this. There's something wildly satisfying in watching raw food become edible in 15 seconds or less.

Pick a song that goes well with the video and, if you can, make sure the camera is in a steady position the whole time, so we can focus on the bread rising and re-rising, loop after loop.

#MarshmallowTest

Test someone and see if they can wait to eat a tempting snack. Kids are best for this as they probably won't realize they're being tested, but you could also try this on an adult.
Place your phone in a discreet location to record the whole experiment. Bake some delicious treats, such as s'mores. Surprise your "subject" by walking up with one fresh s'more on a plate. Ask if they want one, too. If they say, "Yes," leave the s'more in front of them and say you will make them two s'mores but that the one on the plate is yours. Turn your back on them while you make two more s'mores. Wait and see what happens next.

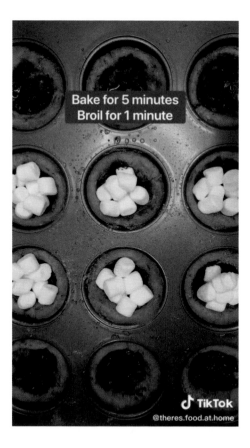

This experiment is perfect for TikTok. Hopefully, they eat the s'more immediately. But if they're patient, good for them! They've earned the two new s'mores.

#NoHandsBake

Bake a cookie with your hands tied behind your back.

#EggDrop

Have an egg-drop competition. Get as many people involved as possible, in teams or as individual competitors. The objective: drop an egg from a very high place (a window, a cliff, a rock-climbing tower, whatever) without it cracking. The egg can be protected only using materials found in your kitchen. Record the different contraptions used to contain the eggs and the individual egg drops. The egg that survives the most drops wins.

Cheat code: place the egg in a jar of peanut butter. I am speaking from experience here.

#HowToCutFood

Create a TikTok montage of food being cut. Pizza being cut with a pizza cutter. Cake being cut with a knife. Steak being sliced up by a steak knife. A huge hunk of meat getting the ax from a butcher's knife. Garlic getting minced. Sugar cookies getting cut out with a cookie cutter. Surely, there can be no more satisfying TikTok.

#TheCandyManCanButShouldHe

Melt a ton of chocolate and cover other food in it. Then eat it. Set the TikTok to a Willy Wonka song, perhaps "The Candy Man Can." There's so much to cover in chocolate: fruit, vegetables, potato chips, nuts, hot dogs*, anything!

*Don't cover meat in chocolate, it's gross.

#StarBaker

Review a baked good as if you are a judge in *The Great British Bake Off*, or any food competition show. There's no need to have any idea what you're talking about, just use realistic terminology ("over-baked," "perfectly risen," "soggy bottom"). Take a bite of something, then take a very long pause—perhaps a comically long 20-second pause—before declaring your expert verdict.

#MegaUltraCheeseburger

Order every fast-food cheeseburger and stack them on top of each other to make the ultra-super-mega-fast-food-cheeseburger. Attempt to take a bite while holding it in both hands. This will be messy!

#ToastTok

Devote thousands of TikToks to toast. Call them ToastToks. Post a video of your toast popping out of the toaster every single day. Try to start recording at a different time each day so we never know when the toast is going to pop up. Every day, people will look forward to their ToastTok.

Review your toast each day as well.

"Today's toast was extra toasty," you might say, or "This toast tasted like burned toast."

#SnowIceCream

If you have snow where you live, consider making your own ice cream with fresh snow. Wait until it's been snowing for a few hours before digging some up. Add evaporated milk, sugar, and vanilla.

There are many recipes online and even more opinions about whether snow ice cream is safe. Ask your doctor if snow ice cream is right for you. If they agree, you may have a pretty cool TikTok on your hands.

#ThePerfectMarshmallow

Attempt to make a perfectly cooked marshmallow for a perfect s'more (brown all over). Record this triumph for a TikTok.

#DeepFriedEverything

Acquire, or get access to, a deep fryer. Fry as many different foods as possible.

#FoodExpectationsVsReality

Duet a food recipe TikTok. Use the duet feature on TikTok to make a side-by-side TikTok of someone else's recipe TikTok. Depending on how it works out, you may be able to caption the duet as "Expectations versus Reality."

#ElaborateGingerbreadHouse

Build an elaborate gingerbread house. The TikTok could be a video showing the construction of the house. You could make a second TikTok, a scripted story about the gingerbread people living in the house. It will likely end in tragedy.

A Gingerbread Sitcom may go something like this:

Fred: George, are you OK?

George: Oh crumbs, what a day.

Fred: What happened?

George: Another co-worker fell in the milk. I don't want to talk about it.

A hand appears out of nowhere, grabbing Fred.

George: Fred, no!

The hand returns Fred. His head is missing.

George: Noooooooo!!!

The story could also be happy, I suppose.

#SameDishAllWeek

Make the same dish every day for a week and see if you improve at making it. Be sure it's something you want to eat every day. It could be a delicious calzone (because no human could dislike a calzone). Take video of that calzone every day and edit the footage together to show your progress throughout the week.

#RanchOrChocolate

Play "ranch or chocolate."

The idea is to say what goes better with a food: ranch dressing or chocolate. For instance, I would say to you, "Oranges," to which you may respond, "Chocolate."

Normally this game is played with just words, but it could go many directions on TikTok. For example, you could make a TikTok asking followers to comment with foods.

Then, video reply to the comments with your choice, ranch or chocolate, and eat that food with ranch or chocolate in the video. Give it a quick review as well ("Mmm, ranch was bad.").

Alternatively, you could test, in real time, what's better for a food. Make it a TikTok Live, if you're feel especially dangerous. Are jelly beans better with chocolate or ranch? The world will finally know, in real time.

#FancyPetFeast

Make an elaborate meal. For a pet.

#OurCookingShow

Start a "cooking show" with a friend or family member. TikTok thrives on community and sharing an experience with someone you're close with really comes through on camera. You'll make memories, and hopefully something delicious, too.

INTERVIEW WITH

BEN DE ALMEIDA
(@Benoftheweek)

Dave Walk me through your process.

Ben Basically, I just write down whatever random story my brain comes up with and then film it. I try and get 50 shots and give myself an hour to edit, so I can add whatever crazy effects and music I want.

Dave How are you editing?

Ben I use Final Cut Pro.

Dave You also have a YouTube channel. Which came first?

Ben YouTube. I've been doing it since I was 10. My channel only became popular after I got a TikTok following. I might do a little story on TikTok and say, "Hey, see the results on YouTube!"

Dave So it was intentional to lead them toward your YouTube?

"You have to leave behind any thought of 'Why is this funny?' It's just a visceral reaction."

Ben Yeah. Incorporating it into these stories was when I started to see growth on YouTube.

Dave Tell me a little about your background.

Ben I had no friends in middle school, so I made a YouTube channel. I'd just hit record, say something in my 10-year-old voice, and upload it.

Dave What was your first TikTok that took off?

Ben It was one where I pretended to microwave a can of beans. People came up to me and were like, "Hey, you put the can of beans in the microwave!"

Dave Have you ever been surprised to get a huge reaction from a TikTok?

Ben There was one where I dropped my cactus and I made a little song and showed it dead on the ground. Months later, I noticed people kept referencing this TikTok. I saw that it had got 20 million views. It's weird, sometimes I'll blow up right away, and sometimes it can take six months.

Dave Why do you think that is?

Ben TikTok gives each video a fair chance. People might not like it right now, but later on they show it to a new group of people who might love it.

Dave How does TikTok continue to evolve?

Ben Well, TikTok is putting a lot of effort into making sure that creators are happy. I can see TikTok as a platform being around for a long time.

Dave Do you have a favorite type of TikTok?

Ben I really like watching cursed memes. Like a frog with like some scary music. Gen Z humor is my favorite type of video on TikTok.

Dave TikTok seems to reflect Gen Z humor. What is Gen Z humor?

Ben You have to leave behind any thought of "Why is this funny?" It's just a visceral reaction.

Dave What's important when making a 60-second TikTok?

Ben You have to really think about it. Otherwise you'll be sitting in front of your camera for 60 seconds not knowing what to do.

Dave What's your favorite all-time TikTok that you've made?

Ben Probably the beans one, because that was the first time I used special effects. So many people believed that I had actually burned my house down.

60-SECOND TIKTOKS

Unlike many other social media platforms that are based on shorter videos, TikTok allows users to shoot up to 59.5 seconds' worth of video.

A TikTok's completion rate is key to its success. If users on the app do not finish a TikTok, the video can begin to lose momentum, until the algorithm ultimately stops pushing the video. So the downside to a longer TikTok is the higher chance of a low completion rate. However, if a longer video engages users the entire time, earning a full completion (or more), the creator is quickly rewarded.

#DramaticStaringContest

Initiate a staring contest. Do NOT blink for 60 seconds. In the caption or in text on screen, encourage users to duet the staring contest.

To add some contrast or excitement, make the background completely chaotic. Put on an explosive action movie and sit right in front of your TV while staring at your phone.

#60SecondNews

Explain a current news event in as much depth as possible in 60 seconds. People actually watch these, especially if the TikTok begins with text, an interesting looking setup, and the phrase "you" is used. Internet video performs better when the word "you" is used in the first few seconds. You should try it.

#TrafficStop

Find a crosswalk that is timed for 60 seconds. Do as many things as possible in the middle of the street in those 60 seconds. Get creative!

#60SecondBook

Storytime! Find a very short children's book and read it in 60 seconds. Be as dramatic as you can, even if the story is not.

189 #TrafficStopForArt

In another 60-second crosswalk-timed TikTok, set up an easel and blank canvas. Paint a picture of one of the cars waiting at the stoplight. Hand the painting to the driver of the car. Run off before they even realize what's happening.

190 #AnotherDayAtWork

Reenact a work meeting and play the part of every character: you, your boss, and your coworkers.

Remember that even seemingly boring day-to-day events or conversations can be funny. After all, that's why TV shows like *The Office* are so successful.

191 #MyPSA

Make a Public Service Announcement about something that matters to you. Speak directly to camera and explain why it matters to you and why you're speaking up about it.

192 #ImportantPSA

Make a PSA (Public Service Announcement) about something silly. Act as if it's serious but it really isn't.

Shoot this in the style of the old NBC "The More You Know" commercials (you can find these on YouTube). Walk slowly into the screen, say your piece, then walk off screen dramatically while a somber tune plays.

193 #InDepthReading

Over-explain the plot of a really simple story in 60 seconds. Really spin it out, as if you're a movie producer turning it into a massive multi-part movie.

The Tortoise and the Hare. In 60 seconds. Go!

#HowItWasMade

Make a discussion-based TikTok. It may be something like, "The brainstorming session that led to Spider-Man" or "The real conversation between Romeo and Juliet," or technically inaccurate TikToks like, "How bean bag chairs were made."

Bean Bag Chair Guy: Hey, so I want to make this new chair.

Furniture Manufacturer: Terrific news, that's what we do best!

BBCG: Really? OK great, because this is a little wild, but I'm positive it will be a super comfortable chair for kids, college students, and adults who share apartments.

FM: Very cool! What is it?

BBCG throws bean bag. FM guy catches it.

BBCG: It's a bean bag.

FM: I'm not following.

BBCG: I want to take that bean bag and make it at least ... twenty times bigger.

FM: Okay ...

BBCG: And that's it.

FM: So, you just want to make a giant bean bag.

BBCG: A giant bean bag CHAIR.

FM: A giant bean bag chair.

BBCG: A giant. Bean bag. Chair.

FM: *(smiling a little now)* A giant bean bag chair.

BBCG nods and smiles.

FM: You've got yourself a deal!

#FiftyNiftyDifferentStates

User @justinpollack7 made a TikTok using the song "Fifty Nifty United States." He jumped back and forth, indicating which states were reopening early during the Coronavirus pandemic and which states were not.

For a less controversial take on this idea, jump back and forth between places you've been to or not been to.

#SilentFilm

Make a TikTok in the style of an old silent movie. A person silently "speaks," followed by a black slide captioning the dialogue text.

#NeighborImpression

Do an impression of someone you knew growing up. It doesn't need to be dead-on and can even be a caricature.

Here's one based on a friend's personal experience.

In my normal voice first

"This is my impression of our nudist next door neighbors who loved to hang out in the nude in their backyard, but didn't want us to freak out and also didn't want us to have to stop playing outside."

actor-y pause before getting into character

"Hey, hey, don't you want to play in the front yard??"

#SecretCarKaraoke

Prop your phone up on the dashboard of a car and sing along to a song with a friend. Don't tell your friend that you're filming. Try to get them to belt out the song. Then reveal you were recording them. Capture their moment of surprise or horror or both. With their permission, upload the results.

#BetterThanTheOriginal

Pick a scene from your absolute favorite movie and lip sync to it. If you're lucky, someone may have already uploaded the whole scene to TikTok already. Piggyback on that audio clip.

#OneFourthMileRun

Try to run around a regulation track in 60 seconds. My congratulations if this is a feat you can actually pull off.

#UlyssesExplained

Try to explain the plot of an extremely long and dense book.

Ulysses. In 60 seconds. Go!

#LifeAtHogwarts

This is one of my personal favorite TikTok trends: create a TikTok showing what it would be like if you were a student at Hogwarts.

Comment on the food, the people, the weird moving stairs. The idea is to just point out the incredibly odd aspects of Hogwarts castle living that are never addressed in the books.

Some examples from if I were a Hogwarts student:

"Are there other sports? We have magic. Surely there are other sports? Dragon polo? Ice hockey where you have to freeze the other team?"

"You're going to fight Voldemort? OK, good luck with that. I am going straight to the kitchen where I can find literally whatever magical food I want."

"The staircases change. Of course I was late to class."

Wear a black robe or sweater and striped tie, play some magical music, and just look generally confused.

#OneShotMusicVideo

Plan a well-choreographed, thought-out music video of a TikTok. Without cutting or stopping the camera, record as many people as possible in a coordinated video that includes dancing, singing, and whatever else you want.

The "long take" is a popular film technique used in movies like *Goodfellas*. In one scene, the characters are moving into different rooms with the camera following them, meaning hundreds of people had to coordinate their movements.

You don't need to be on Martin Scorsese directing levels, but working to create one flawless scene is a very effective way of stretching your producing and directing muscles. And people will notice! If it's really well done, they may not notice right away, but a well-made TikTok and a good "long take" almost always get appreciated in time.

#FireplaceLoop

Record a fireplace or campfire for 60 seconds. It worked for a four-hour yule log "movie," which used to be shown every holiday season in the US. It should work for a TikTok, too.

#WorkingOutIsMyThing

If working out is your thing, show off your best 60 second workout. Fitness TikToks are HUGE and often promoted by TikTok on the Discover page.

#WorkingOutIsNotMyThing

If working out is not your thing, make up a fake exercise and show it off in 60 seconds or less.

"The key here is to lift your coffee mug in a continuous motion while engaging your triceps and eating a chocolate bar simultaneously. Do you feel it?"

#WhatHair

Buzz your hair in sixty seconds or less. Only do this if it's something you were planning to do. The before and after of buzzed hair is intriguing and kind of addictive.

#EvolutionOfTikTok

In the style of the original viral YouTube hit "the evolution of dance," take us through the "evolution of Tiktok" since its beginning a short time ago. Perform as many memes as possible in 60 seconds.

Users have often made long TikToks that make as many references to other TikToks as possible. See @speechieais's TikTok that includes no fewer than a dozen classic TikTok references in about 45 seconds.

#MyPyramidScheme

Make up a "pyramid scheme" and present it to your "investors" on TikTok. The scheme could be as simple as encouraging your followers to like your video, then they go and tell two other people to like your video, then those two people tell four people to like your TikToks, and on and on.

Take your time to explain this scheme as if it's totally normal and a real business model. Importantly, make sure to wear business attire and have a white board or easel with a chart showing "profits going up!"

Together, we can help you get more likes.

#MomDadHelpMe

Record yourself calling your parents and asking them for TikTok ideas.

#100Shots

Make a TikTok that has more than 100 different shots edited together.

#WordsPerMinutes

See how many words you can type in a minute. There are many online tests that keep track of your WPM. Challenge your followers to beat your record.

#WordsPerMinutePerOneFinger

Do the Words Per Minute challenge but this time just using one finger. It's so hard!

#TallestPersonAlive

Become the tallest person alive by sitting on a friend's shoulder (or vice versa) in a trench coat. Record this journey.

#WhenToHeimlich

If you have taken a class and are certified, make a detailed TikTok showing how the Heimlich maneuver is performed. It's probably safest to demonstrate this on a stuffed animal or a pillow instead of a real person.

 ## #MyReview

Review something. A book, a new movie, a new smart phone, a relative of yours, anything! Really get into what makes this thing good or bad and award it on a points system of your own creation.

INTERVIEW WITH
THE MCFARLANDS
(@the.mcfarlands)

Dave You've mastered what I think works so well on TikTok—authenticity. What is your process?

Colin I do the shooting and editing on my iPhone. Even though it's a 15-second video, I want it to feel like you're actually here in our kitchen with us. When it's done, I'll send it in the family group chat.

Dave Do certain people have critiques?

Colin [laughs] Mom's always the first one to reply and she's just like, "My boys are so handsome." The honest feedback, I get from Dylan.

Dave How do you come up with a TikTok?

Dan A lot of our material is funny stuff we do around the house and we put a spin on it.

Colin Our content is something that could really happen. Like when you have the perfect dap handshake and it just explodes.

"People watch us and think, 'I can do this with my family.'"

Dave How would you describe your TikToks?

Dylan There are three tiers. Level one is basic: like we're all in the kitchen and we start singing a jingle. Then the next level is a situation we might ad lib.

Colin But there's no story behind it.

Dylan And then the third level is a well-thought-out story. Colin writes a script, like a scene from a movie.

Dave Would you say it's an accurate representation of your family?

Dylan Yes, 100%. We went to a couple of creator conventions, and people were like, "You're the exact same people."

Colin And a lot of people recognized his face [points at Dan], because how many times do you see a guy with a gray beard on TikTok?

Dave I want to know more about Dan...

Dan I grew up in a family of seven kids and my parents were a blast. And with these guys, we always had a blast even before TikTok, too.

Dave Is there a Tier 1 TikTok that surprised you when it took off?

Colin Yeah, Mom bought this sauce called "Pineapple Huli Huli" sauce. We did a TikTok around that and it got half a million likes.

Dylan Yeah, and the very first one that absolutely blew up for us was Dad standing by the oven. He just screams...

Dan ..."What's for dinner?"

Dylan Yeah, that one got a million views in no time.

Dave What has been the most rewarding part of growing your account?

Colin Channel growth and seeing how many people are actually commenting, "I love this family."

Dylan People watch us and think, "I can do this with my family."

Dan For me, it's the time spent with those guys. It's family time.

Dave Why is TikTok better than other apps?

Colin Nothing feels as authentic as TikTok.

Dylan Yeah, and TikTok truly cares about its creators.

Dave Could you all give me your TikTok prompt for the book?

Colin We always thought it would be hysterical to show what people are doing once the cameras cut on reality shows. I can't stop thinking that there's someone holding a camera in this person's face. Sometimes, it ruins TV for me.

WHOLESOME TIKTOKS

Wholesome TikTok is characterized by videos that make the viewer feel all warm and fuzzy inside. These videos should come from the heart. Many wholesome videos on TikTok weren't originally intended to be wholesome when they were posted, or at least they weren't trying to earn fake internet points. It's just people who put something out there in good faith and rightfully earned some attention. Make a TikTok in the spirit of putting something positive out into the world, and you're well on your way to wholesomeness.

 ## #DanceClass

Make a TikTok with an older relative. It could be teaching them a dance move or simply trying to explain a current meme to them. If possible, record them secretly for a genuine reaction. Make sure to get their permission to post it, of course.

 ## #TheMostBeautifulThingISawToday

Talk about something beautiful you saw today. It might be a human interaction. It could be an especially beautiful plant or sunset. Maybe it was just a really nice movie. Explain how it made you feel. Don't put any music behind it—the less manufactured your story feels, the more people will connect.

 ## #FreeCompliments

Give out compliments to people and record their reactions. This is a concept that's been around since way before TikTok. I can't imagine doing this little experiment wouldn't make you smile and feel a little happy yourself, too. Great hair today, by the way.

 ## #BalloonHigh

Attach something small to as many balloons as possible. Record the moment it has enough balloons to actually hover. Play something like the *Up* soundtrack behind it.

Um, don't do this with dogs—unless it's indoors, I suppose.

#NewHobby

Pick up a new hobby and record yourself getting better at it every day. When you're finally at a milestone you hoped to reach, edit all of that footage together into one short TikTok that quickly shows the progress you made over time.

Want to start with an easy skill? Try juggling or flipping a coin over and under your knuckles like Jack Sparrow. I practice that every time I'm watching TV and now I have nowhere to show off this impressive, useless skill except for TikTok.

#AFewOfTheirFavoriteThings

Go up to someone and say all of their favorite things. Ask if they want to do those things today. Record their reaction this whole time as their face lights up more and more.

This meme originated with users saying words their dog knew to get them especially excited. For instance, "Do you want to go to the PARK to get TREATS and then get in the CAR to see your GRANDMA and other DOGS?" Dogs freaked out and literally drooled as their owner put extra emphasis on their favorite words.

Later, users started doing this but with their partners ("Do you want to go to the MALL and see a MOVIE then buy some ICE CREAM then later watch your FAVORITE TV SHOW?").

Pick your lucky victim and arm yourself with all of their favorite things to do. But make sure you follow through with your promises, or the TikTok will be cursed.

#RealLifeUp

Tell a wholesome real-life romantic story. It could be about you and your partner, or your parents, or just a real neat couple down the street. Incorporate old pictures, videos, and testimonials from the partners. Explain how you know these people and what their love means to you.

#SameLookButOlder

Use the Simple Plan "I'm Just a Kid" song and show old, awkward pictures of yourself. The easiest and most visually pleasing way to execute this meme is by positioning yourself the same way you were in the photo, even wearing similar clothing items. Then, as soon as you are directly mirroring the former you, cut to the picture.

#KidsReview

Ask a young daughter, son, niece, nephew, or younger sibling to give a movie review of their favorite movie. Let them go on as long as they want, then clip the best parts together in a TikTok. Put music from the movie's soundtrack quietly behind it. Make sure they rate the movie out of five stars.

#SneakHugAttack

"Sneak-hug" people you care about. Make sure they don't know you're recording so you can capture a real, hopefully warm reaction.

 ### #UnderratedAccounts

Make a TikTok complimenting another, lesser-known, TikTok account. Point out your favorite TikToks they've made, what you really like about them, and why other people should follow them. When I first started out, this was the absolute best type of TikTok to be tagged in. The handful of times it happened completely renewed my energy and self-confidence.

 ### #FamilyReaction

Have someone in your family react to an especially strange, but popular, TikTok video. Use the Duet or React feature to record them watching.

 ### #ParentingUpsAndDowns

If you're a parent, or a pet parent, make a TikTok about the ups and downs of raising children, cats, dogs, or fish.

 ### #SnoreTrack

Record someone snoring and sing along softly to it.

 ### #PregnantTimeLapse

If you or somebody you know is pregnant (and is happy to share their journey), record their progress over time in a photo montage, ending with the baby in their arms. Awwww!

 ### #TheirFavoriteSong

Sneak up on someone and blast the best part of their favorite song. Record their (hopefully) delighted reaction.

#PureYourMamaJokes

Create a back-and-forth skit in which you sling "your mama" jokes at another person. Except instead of insults, they're really wholesome compliments. For added emphasis, include the sound of other people making dramatic "ooooooh" sounds every time a compliment is dropped.

Person One: Your mama is so delightful, she once asked me if I was thirsty, then brought me back four different drink options!

Crowd: OOOOooooooh!

Person Two: Oh yeah? Well your mama is so wonderful, I often hope that I grow up to be as caring and thoughtful as her!

Crowd: OH NO HE DID NOT!

Person One: Well your mama is so supportive, you grew up to be a well-adjusted human!

Person Two: Thanks, man.

#PleaseTakeASeat

Wait for your roommate or partner to get home. Be seated quietly at one end of a table. Have a single glass of wine or other singular beverage for extra effect. Wear a very grim look on your face. Ask them to sit down.

Once seated, start with, "We need to talk," then say something ridiculous, unimportant, or a secret compliment:

- We need to talk about you not replacing the toilet paper roll.
- We need to talk about how much time you spend on TikTok. Your videos are awesome.
- We need to talk about you being such a great dresser. Where do you buy your shirts?

#InsideJokesExplained

Pick the most obscure inside joke in your family or group of friends and try to explain it in a TikTok.

#HumanVsCartoon

Perform various actions, then perform them as a cartoon would. This TikTok trend has seen users miming walking into doors, sneezing, or stepping on a banana peel, and then repeating the same action in an exaggerated cartoon fashion.

 ### #BackyardCamping

Go camping in the woods or your backyard and record some of the setup and the fire at night. Don't record every moment though—enjoy the outdoors!

 ### #FamilyTraditions

Record your family sitting down to eat at a holiday. Maybe you want to show the quirkiest family tradition, or highlight all of the "characters" of your family. Memorialize the moment not just for TikTok but also for yourself to look back on years later.

 ### #ADayEarly

Come home a day early from a trip and surprise a loved one with your (hopefully missed) presence.

If your presence wasn't missed, post that TikTok anyway. That's pretty funny. Maybe not for you...

 ### #MyFamilyTree

Tell the story of your family tree. Use plenty of photographs and graphics if you can. If you're not video-graphic-savvy, make a physical family tree with clearly labeled notecards. Explain when and why people moved to a different house or emigrated to another country. Point out your favorite relative on the family tree and explain what makes them so awesome.

#JingleTrivia

Start singing a well-known commercial jingle to someone who often sings whatever they hear. See if they finish the jingle on their own.

For example, "Oh I wish I were an Oscar Meyer Weiner ..."

This idea is dedicated to my grandpa, who used to collaborate with me on picking a song we could whistle that would prompt my dad to absentmindedly start singing the song. Every time.

 ## #CheckingIn

Use the audio "Right Back Where We Started From." You'll find that this audio has thousands of videos in which people are just smiling at the camera. The text typically says something like, "Just me and my future best friend staring at each other."

Make your own version of that relevant to whatever is happening in your life, others, or out in the world. It's a great way to invite duets from other TikTok users in the most wholesome way possible.

 ## #WeAllMakeMistakes

Use the "EverybodyMakesMistakes" audio and highlight a moment you did something you're embarrassed by.

Example:

Dave to camera now smiling sheepishly and mouthing, "Everybody makes mistakes."

Meanwhile, the text on screen reads, "I don't want to cut my hair but I'll let my older sister cut me some bangs."

Cut to the picture of my slanted bangs haircut in middle school that my sister accidentally gave me.

(Based on true events.)

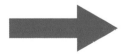

#TinyTales

Collaborate with a kid to tell a made-up story, and illustrate it with their drawings. If they want to, let them create the storyline and narrate it.

#FlowersForYou

Give someone the biggest bouquet of flowers they've ever received. Record their reaction.

#GrandparentTikTok

Encourage your grandparents to start a TikTok account, or start one for them. Create posts with them and they can reply to comments. Grandparent TikTok is so heartwarming that it deserves its own chapter, and all the ideas would be something like "Capture your grandpa retelling a favorite family moment or memory." Pure wholesome gold.

#CozySweaterWeather

Find the coziest song imaginable. It could be a Taylor Swift break-up, sweater-wearing kind of song. Or a more uplifting wintertime holiday season song. Just sit in front of a fire with a cup of coffee, tea, or hot cocoa for 15 seconds while this song plays. The idea is to create a cozy environment that makes the viewer want to throw on a sweater immediately, even in June.

INTERVIEW WITH
JACK CORBETT
(@planetmoney)

Dave Who exactly launched the Planet Money TikTok account?

Jack The NPR video team makes Planet Money Shorts, which are five-to-eight minute explainers about economics concepts. All the TikToks were based off of episodes. What happened was it became my turn to make one of those. The stock market was going crazy and we were talking about what kind of videos the world needs and one of my good friends Chanti said, "I just want to watch a slow-motion video of water or concentric circles, something chill." And I was like, "That's what the stock market circuit breaker is. It's just trying to get you to chill out." So I made a three-minute horizontal video. Can you imagine? And then they said, "Just make it 59 seconds and vertical." That's how it all started.

Dave And what is your background?

"It's not going to look perfect, so you might as well just embrace that."

Jack I started a year ago as the music video intern. Then I bounced around just to try and see what else was working, and they were all super accommodating. I started to sit in on the meetings for those older Planet Money Short videos.

Dave What is your involvement with each TikTok?

Jack I shoot them, I direct them. [laughs] Direct them—I set the plastic tripod up. I'll write the whole concept, I'll bounce it off my supervisor, and she'll help to refine it. And then I shoot, I edit, I do all the animations for the ones that I make. There's several other people on the team who make them as well.

Dave I'd say your aesthetic is usually an '80s video game vibe, but what would you call it?

Jack It's janky. [both laugh] All the animations are not supposed to flow. It's not going to look perfect, so you might as well just embrace that.

Dave Where does a TikTok start for you?

Jack Most of them are based off of Planet Money episodes. So with my "Middle Man" TikTok—the process was strange. I went through this episode that illustrated what "middle men" are and how the Internet is changing what that means.

Dave What is more important—quantity or quality?

Jack It's got be quality, but to my undoing because that is a perfectionist thing. I don't think we've ever had to get something out that's relevant to something that's happening right now. We do have topical things, but we always go through our system of approvals for stuff, making sure the script is totally accurate.

Dave Do you ever know beforehand if a TikTok is going to go viral?

Jack I never know what's going to be a big one. But in times like those, quantity sometimes helps. If you're stuck on one, you know what? There will be three more next week.

Dave What's a fun TikTok explainer idea?

Jack Find an absolutely random thing on the Internet and, if you relate to it in any way, at least a dozen other people will, too. Explain that thing but always keep in mind how it made you feel. Try and translate that feeling, that mood into the video.

Dave How would you describe the TikTok community?

Jack It's probably people who get slightly less sleep than their counterparts. I mean, people who are scrolling a bit too much. That's the best characterization I could make.

Dave That's my favorite answer, hands down.

EXPLAINER TIKTOKS

Ranging from serious news events to hilarious off-beat, but informative videos, Explainer TikTok is the perfect launch pad to generate interest in complicated topics.

If it sounds like you're experiencing a particularly weird dream while reading these prompts, that's kind of what it's like to watch the TikToks too. And yet—you learn something!

 ### #MacroVsMicro

Make a TikTok explaining the difference between macroeconomics and microeconomics. When talking about macroeconomics, hold the phone lower and have it angled up at you to make yourself appear larger. For microeconomics, do the opposite and hold the camera up high above you, making yourself look smaller.

 ### #LOTRexplained

Explain the plot of *Lord of the Rings* or any other dense book in less than 60 seconds. Speak as quickly as possible and cut out any breaths or pauses. Hopefully, no one uses your summary to avoid reading a book for class, but if they are, at least they'll learn something.

 ### #PlantCare

It's a long-running joke that many young people do not have kids but do have plants. And often, those plants die. Research the art of keeping plants alive and make TikToks describing how to take care of individual plants. Does an aloe plant need sunlight? Do I ever need to trim it? Should I sing to it? Should I make TikToks with it in which we are both singing karaoke? You know, the normal plant questions.

#SelfReflection

Make a TikTok explaining something that you yourself recently learned about. This could be a great space to talk about social issues and how they intersect with your life, and to reflect on ways in which you can be a more supportive person.

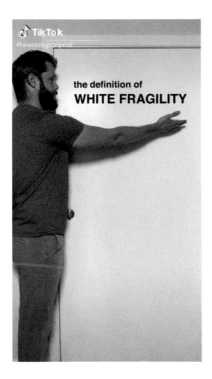

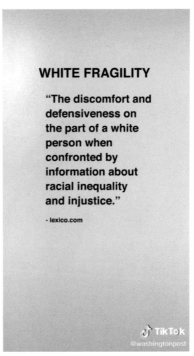

#WordOfTheDay

Define an interesting new word you just learned, giving the etymology of the word if you can. Maybe your whole TikTok account could become a dictionary account, introducing a new word every day.

#HowToChangeCarOil

Show how to change the oil of a car by yourself. I would personally love to see a TikTok on this, because I have no idea.

#GoodLightingMatters

Make a TikTok explaining the importance of good lighting. Show what you use to get good light in your TikToks—whether it's natural light outside, big windows, an expensive studio light, or a single lightbulb dangling from the ceiling that makes your TikToks super creepy.

#VacuumsSuck

Find a vacuum that you're comfortable dismantling and rebuilding and use it to explain how vacuums work. Sure, we know they suck up dirt, but how? Why are dogs afraid of them? There's so much to explore in the realm of vacuums and their suckiness.

#FillOutACheck

Find the image of a check online (definitely not your own!) and use this to explain how a checking account works. What's the first number? What's the second number? Why do the numbers look weird? Do checks expire? How can one little piece of paper hold so much power? Half of those questions are still a mystery to me so, please, answer them.

#HowToChangeATire

Demonstrate how to change a car's tire. With efficient editing and timing, this could be explained in less than 60 seconds and may be a huge help to someone who finds themselves stranded with only a spare tire and TikTok for help.

#TikTokAlgorithmExplained

Explain how the TikTok algorithm works. Here's some information to get you started:

- When you first log on to TikTok, you're shown eight videos from a variety of people and topics.

- Based off of your likes, time spent watching the video, and commenting, the algorithm begins to show you videos related to the ones you engaged with most.

- TikTok then shows you videos from "clusters" that have similar themes.

- The algorithm avoids videos that are too similar and will not necessarily show you a TikTok that has the same audio as another TikTok you like.

- You may get stuck in a "filter bubble" only showing you the same type of content you initially liked. To avoid this, you need to proactively search for different content, either in the search bar or on the Discover page.

There's no better group of people to talk about TikTok with than the users on the app.

 #HowToHangThings

Make a TikTok about home repair or decorating, such as how to hang a picture. Make it attention-grabbing from the start by opening with you drilling through a wall.

 #BehindTheScenes

Explain how you make your TikToks. Whether it's complicated or easy, you will find that people are usually interested in the behind-the-scenes of creating something.

#HowToFileTaxes

File your taxes, or talk about filing your taxes, on TikTok. This is admittedly an odd idea for an app largely used by young people who have no need to file taxes. But those people will one day grow up and files taxes. Not to mention, there's been a huge increase of Millennials, Gen X, and, yes, even the elusive Boomers on TikTok. Hopefully the Boomers already know how to file taxes, but it's never too late to learn. Take inspiration from the time TurboTax did a marketing campaign on TikTok featuring the Turbo Tax Dance.

#ShaveYourFaceOff

Demonstrate how to shave. It could be your face, could be your legs—whatever tickles your fancy, or whatever is currently tickling your skin.

#NailGrowth

Why do nails grow faster for some people and slower for others? What do we eat that makes them grow? Research this and explain it while cutting yours nails.

#FoldAPlane

Look up a unique paper airplane design you've never made before, master it, then make a TikTok showing how to fold it. TikTok's natural vertical video format is perfect for paper airplane folding, which conveniently starts with a vertical piece of rectangular paper.

#MakeYourOwnFont

How is a font made? Can anyone make a font? Where do they submit it? Make a TikTok exploring this process.

so I wanted to turn my handwriting into a font...

so I filled this chart out

& uploaded this sheet

and I LOVE IT.

hello, this is my standard handwr|

103

#SurvivalFire

Demonstrate how to build a fire with just dry wood, flint, and steel, a pair of thick glasses, or even two sticks (which, by the way, is almost impossible). This is an essential camping skill that few truly know how to do.

#HowFiresStart

In a follow-up TikTok, explain the science behind fire. Why does a fire need oxygen? What chemical reaction is actually happening and why is it called "combustion"?

#ConnectTheStars

There are several great apps that use the phone's position to point out exactly where stars are, even if it's the middle of the day and they aren't visible to you. Pick a star or constellation at random and explain how it was given that name.

#DopamineHit

Use dialogue and visuals to demonstrate what makes social media so addictive. What's happening in our brains?

Dave: OK, TikTok posted!

Dave sits with his phone, watching the reactions come in.

Dave: Oh my god! People love it! It has so many views already!

The camera zooms into Dave's head.

We cut to a dark room. Text on screen says, "Dave's dopamine." Dopamine Dave is inside, representing the brain.

Dopamine Dave: OH WE LIKE THIS! I am releasing pleasure! Get more viral hits and I will release more of the dopamine!

The camera zooms out of Dave's head.

Dave: I've got to make another viral TikTok immediately.

#WhereToRecycle

Research how various materials are recycled in your area. Why recycling? Because TikTok loves the planet and you should too.

You can learn about local recycling online by searching your town or city's recycling center, or asking the people who collect it.

Dave (talking to camera): Where does your recycled stuff go? I asked the person who picks it up.

Dave outside with person who picks it up.

Dave: Where does it go?

Guy: I dunno. To the recycling center.

Dave: And how quickly is it recycled?

Guy: Call the center and find out.

Dave: Cool!

Cut to Dave calling the recycling center and learning on speaker phone about the distribution of recycled goods.

#EpisodeRecap

Break down weekly episodes of your favorite TV show. Target a show's devoted followers by posting limmediate reaction TikToks. Make sure to post them every week at the same time so followers know when to expect new recaps.

#WhatTimeIsIt

What are time zones and why do we have them? Make a TikTok about the time zones the entire world agreed to. Or talk about how the Internet and globalization in general have some people calling for one universal clock.

#ClimateCrisisIsReal

What is the climate crisis? Make a series of longer TikToks going into detail, or a single TikTok focusing on the basics.

 #FindTheBalance

Explain "white balance" on a camera and how it works. In the edit, adjust the white balance to show why a white sheet of paper is important for finding white balance.

 #EmojiSubmissions

Where do emojis come from? It turns out there's a committee that decides what emojis to add to all the major keyboards. Make a TikTok about this approval process and ask followers what emoji they want to be invented.

 #SimilarBeliefs

Explain the similarities between some religions. Remember to be respectful of people's beliefs.

 #Cameras101

If you're a photographer, make a series of TikToks explaining how different aspects of a camera work. What's a long lens? What's a wide lens? What's the lens on my phone? All of these questions could be individual TikToks that help you grow a following of first-time photographers.

INTERVIEW WITH
IAN MCKENNA
(@nowthispolitics)

Dave What's your experience been like on TikTok?

Ian There's truly not an algorithm as specifically curated for you as this one is.

Dave How did you get assigned to the NowThis Politics TikTok?

Ian They made an account without telling me, and they handed me the password and said, "You were good at Vine. You should figure out how to do this. Everybody's doing it. Dave's doing it. You could do it. No problem."

Dave You're the only person I'm aware of, besides me, who did News Vines and now is doing News TikToks. We can form a very small little club. Are you surprised by the engagement you get?

"If you are able to speak truth to power, I think that's something that's always going to be appreciated, especially by a younger audience."

Ian I think what Gen Z brings to TikTok is a very open spirit of debate. On TikTok there are all of these people, either in my comments or in my feed, all wanting to have a conversation. They're truly trying to find out how the world works. I think people underestimate what goes on on TikTok.

Dave I saw you published a clip from the 2016 presidential debate, where Trump is talking about his taxes. Do you think there's value in Archival Footage TikTok?

Ian My favorite thing about my job is archival footage. I love digging through stuff. For example, I was reading *The New Yorker* and they had a quote [from 2002] from a State Senator in Florida, who was trying to clamp down on voter registration in Florida. In this quote, he was saying that it should be harder to vote because people died for our right to vote. So I spent a whole afternoon digging through Florida's Senate archives for this clip from 2002. I posted it and people went just as bananas as I did, which was really reaffirming. There's a symbiosis between anger and hopefulness that I hope to convey sometimes.

Dave How do you decide how to format a clip?

Ian The three-box method I use was one of the things where there is so much happening in the entire frame, it feels like a cheat to give somebody just a little bit. My preference is to see everything that's going on, all the time. So when I'm making a White House press briefing video, you get to see who's asking the question, and who's answering the question. There's a lot of opportunity to show way more than people normally get to see.

Dave If someone were to start an account right now with the intention of it being politically focused, what kind of advice would you give them?

Ian I think the world needs a lot of fact-checking right now, and I've found that the audience on TikTok is really receptive to fact-checking because in a way, it is very high drama, catching somebody in a lie. So, if somebody was trying to get into Political TikTok, I would say focus on things you can easily call out. If you are able to speak truth to power, I think that that's something that's always going to be appreciated, especially by a younger audience.

Dave Could you give me an idea for a TikTok somebody could make?

Ian Sure! If there's an idea about politics that you don't understand, teach it to yourself and then try to teach it to everybody else on TikTok. Some people don't know the things they don't know yet. So it's super helpful if you find something you don't know, teach it to yourself, and then put it out there for other people. Another pitch would be, research one politician you dislike and find one thing you agree with them about. I think that that might be helpful for everybody's sake to find some common ground with people.

POLITICAL TIKTOKS

For the politically active users of TikTok, the app itself happens to be a pretty good platform for discussions, rants, explainers, and more.

When thinking about making a Political TikTok, what should be the goal? I believe informing others and provoking rational conversations is a good start—at least while TikTok is still a relatively wholesome place.

 #AllTheParties

Describe the different political parties in your country. Explain how each party feels about a particular topic. For example, one might use taxes to explain the two major parties, or the differing stances of the Libertarian and Green Party.

 #PoliticalSongs

Pick a song associated with politics and explain its origins and how it came to represent a person or party. Play that song in the background.

For example, "The Washington Post March" is often used for events involving the U.S. president. Far more people recognize the song than know its name. It turns out the name is very literal. The early owners of the *Washington Post* in the late 1880s paid famous composer John Phillip Sousa to write the song. Over the years, it's become more synonymous with the president than the newspaper that paid for its creation.

 #PointingForVotes

Show the different ways politicians use their hands and gestures, whether it be pointing with a flattened thumbs-up, or raising their arms frantically. Use text to indicate the politician you are imitating. Don't speak at all and consider putting music underneath. This TikTok should be entirely about body language.

281 #DebateNightClips

There are plenty of live television political events, such as debates, that seem to be created for knee-jerk reactions. Show the clip on the screen by filming it on your TV, then quickly flip the camera around and give your reaction and thoughts. Do this in a straightforward way, or add a funny spin. For example, a "debate night bingo" game, where you call bingo when a politician has said certain buzzwords.

282 #PoliticalMashups

Make a TikTok that smashes together real moments in politics with songs or movie clips. Back during the 2016 U.S. presidential election, Vine was alive and well (R.I.P.). It was in this time that I learned to edit video using the platform and made Vine clips of debate moments and other political milestones. Within minutes, we would have the clip of a debate on Vine, with a sliver of a pop culture reference added in. We went as far as setting "sad" debate moments for a politician to emotional Dashboard Confessional songs.

#AllThePresidentsDrinks

Do a mini TikTok series on the preferred drinks of political figures. Add some extra humor to it by pretending to be the politician enjoying their drink of choice.

#WhatsThisProtestFor

Post a montage of photos and pictures from a recent protest. Explain in accompanying text what the protest was about and what the protests hoped to achieve.

#ThisWasARealAd

Find an old political ad and re-create it shot for shot. Use the same audio.

#PoliticalHumor

Conservatives and liberals often accuse each other of not being funny. Wherever you fall politically, put an end to this debate by making a TikTok. Start with "I am a [conservative, liberal, something] and I am here to prove we are funny," then tell the worst dad joke you can find.

#NewPerspective

Make a TikTok interviewing someone about a political issue that they know a lot about and are happy to give their perspective on. I made a TikTok with my colleague Jonathan Capehart where I asked him about systemic racism. His thoughtful answer made for an informative video.

#VoteForMe

Create your own political ad. It can have a real platform or a fake platform, but try hard to make it feel like a real ad. Shake hands with fellow "constituents," use a voice-over explaining your message, come up with a slogan and slap it on the end, and just generally really overdo it.

 #SpeechContradictions

Find a moment when a politician contradicted themselves. Play the two clips back-to-back. Use text to show when both statements were said.

 #PoliticianLipSync

Pull up a recording of a politician, recent or old, and lip sync to their words. Sarah Cooper first broke out on TikTok by mouthing run-on sentences from President Trump.

#HowToTeleprompt

The teleprompter is a long-standing punchline when talking about U.S. presidents.

Cast yourself as a politician reading a teleprompter. Cut back and forth between yourself and the "prompter." It can just be a person holding a sheet of paper with large, bold text.

Politician: And from here on out, I promise you can always count on me.

Cut to "Teleprompter" holding up those exact lines.

Politician: Seriously, just call me. My number is 202-4835 ...

Teleprompter with new sign "DON'T GIVE OUT YOUR NUMBER!"

Politician: Whoops! Just kidding. Never call me. I will never be around.

Teleprompter's sign now says, "NO! YOU'LL ALWAYS BE AROUND!"

Politician: I mean, I'll always be around. Party at my house. Everyone come on over!

Teleprompter hangs his head, dejected.

#WhatPoliticiansGoogle

Pick a politician and pull up their Google results page. Screenshot or video record this on your phone, set up the Green Screen effect and pop up in front of the results. Ask your followers to comment as if they are that politician Googling questions. The first example of this meme saw people suggesting what U.K. Prime Minister Boris Johnson might Google. Most users will take this as an opportunity to poke fun at the chosen politician—that's politics for you.

#BritishParliamentInRealLife

Re-create the British Parliament but for a normally relaxed event. The text on screen could be, "If eating dinner was like the British Parliament."

Dave sits down at dinner table.

Parent: You're late.

Dave: I am not.

Parent suddenly stands up, red in the face, yelling.

Parent: YES YOU ARE!

The table erupts in chaos as everyone suddenly stands and yells at each other in all directions.

#IdeologiesAtTheGroceryStore

Take an everyday scenario and show how a conservative, liberal, libertarian, and socialist would deal with it. A grocery store might be a fun place for this.

#NewPoliticalTerm

Take a recent term that has entered the political zeitgeist and define it. Put the whole definition in text and read out the definition. Provide an example of this phrase in the TikTok.

#WhoSaidIt

Choose a series of quotes from two opposing political figures and read them out loud. Give the viewer a moment to guess which figure said the quote before pointing to the person.

#TheTikTokParty

Create a new political party on TikTok. Give it a memorable name and try to recruit others to join your party.

298 #DanceForAwareness

If there's an issue that you particularly care about, or some information that you want to make sure people know about, use the power of dance to get your message out there. User @lauralouiserice created a TikTok of her dancing while the message "please register to vote" was displayed on the screen.

please register to vote

♪ TikTok
@lauralouiserice

#ParodyComparison

If you are edit-savvy, take a clip of a politician being imitated on a popular show like *Saturday Night Live* and stack it on top of a clip of the actual politican saying the same lines. Way back in 2016, a colleague of mine did this in a Vine to great effect.

#PartySongs

Play various songs associated with political parties. Invite the viewers to guess if the party is liberal or conservative. Wait a few seconds for each song before revealing its political slant.

#ModelUN

If you are an active member of Model U.N., record the roleplay that goes into a Model U.N. convention.

#ClimateCrisisDenierDenier

The topic of the climate crisis is in TikTok's DNA. In the app's early days, you couldn't make it through five TikToks without seeing a "VSCO Girl" urging viewers to reuse straws, save the turtles, and drink out of a Hydro Flask.

Make a TikTok that gives pointers for how to argue with someone who doesn't believe the climate crisis is real. Give examples of questions someone might ask, and supply answers that your viewers can use in their next online debate.

#NewMoneyFace

Explain why you think a political figure should replace another on a form of currency.

#WhoCelebritiesSupport

Pull up pictures of celebrities and make a montage showing what political party each one supports. Make sure each celebrity has declared their support publicly, first.

#HowCaucusesWork

Explain how a caucus works with a TikTok showing your friends or family participating in a caucus to decide what to eat for dinner. Feature commentary from pretend cable news hosts. Announce a winner.

#UnitedNationsMeeting

Pretend to be a country at the United Nations that's just trying to get a small goal achieved while the other countries mess it up. Play the parts of the different global powers quarreling while your country is just hoping for a nice box seat at the next Olympics. As they keep fighting, your country gets more and more drowned out.

#HistoricalContext

Compare a historical event to something happening right now. Show the similarities and differences. Don't skimp on details but don't dramatize it either. Sometimes, all people need is context to understand the significance of a modern-day event.

#DeepDivisionsExplained

Take a divisive political event and explain all sides. Ask your followers to comment what they think, and who they side with. Attempt to be cordial in your responses.

#ElectoralCollegeExplained

Make a TikTok to explain the Electoral College.

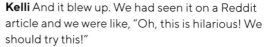

VISUAL EFFECTS TIKTOKS

INTERVIEW WITH

KELLI AND FREEMAN
(@happykelli)

Dave The first TikTok of yours I saw had Kelli's body parts flying everywhere. In fact, I ended up "borrowing" that idea. Were you the first to do that?

Kelli Actually we were not the first ones.

Freeman That was our first video though.

Kelli And it blew up. We had seen it on a Reddit article and we were like, "Oh, this is hilarious! We should try this!"

Dave Walk me through your TikTok process.

Freeman Normally it comes up while I'm falling asleep. I'm just like, "Oh this would be funny!" or "I saw this, how can we make it our own?"

Kelli If there's dance involved, we'll choose a song that goes with it and then I'll come up with some sort of choreography to go with it. We don't do a lot of storyboarding or planning. We just go with the flow. A lot of times we'll film in a bunch of different outfits, which can be tricky because you have to be so precise. You have to be fast because we don't have a lot of lighting equipment. Then Freeman will take all the footage and edit it in Adobe Premiere.

"Don't sweat the small stuff. Post things that you may not be proud of because who knows?"

Freeman Normally, when we fly to space it's because the dancing doesn't match up perfectly or the video is kind of boring. It's not planned.

Dave What is your favorite part of TikTok?

Kelli I love Old Grandma TikTok. I always love the old people and the babies doing funny things.

Dave Is there any other TikTok that surprised you by how it just took off?

Kelli The TikTok that we made that I'm appearing out of the box, moonwalk, and then go back into the box. We just made that on a whim.

Freeman I'm not a professional editor. In the box video, the editing is not that good. The shadows on the wall are bad and it's not convincing that she's coming out of the box. I was blown away that it got millions of views.

Dave Do you shoot all of them on a smart phone?

Freeman Yeah. We're not fancy.

Kelli Yeah, if it's too professional, then it doesn't come across well.

Dave Have you found a caption that really worked?

Freeman If there's something that happens later in the video and it's an exciting thing, I normally just say, "Wait until the surprise at 15 seconds."

Dave What is your favorite all-time TikTok you've made?

Kelli The one dancing to "You Spin Me Right Round, Baby." I love just dancing deadpan to the camera.

Freeman Kelli is a professional dancer. She danced on Broadway.

Dave Do you have any advice for new TikTok creators?

Freeman Don't sweat the small stuff. Post things that you may not be proud of because who knows? And no one will see it if it's not good.

Dave OK, your turn to provide a prompt for the book.

Freeman We have a video where she walked into the kitchen and then we turn the corner and she's walking back up behind the couch. Have your subject mime walking downstairs behind something. Then film a shot with no one there, so you can make it look like they disappear in the edit. Then shoot turning to another spot, so your subject can walk back up the stairs behind a couch or a table.

VISUAL EFFECTS TIKTOKS

TikTok has a community of creators using visual effects to tell stories. Creators can utilize hundreds of totally unique and often technologically mind-boggling in-app effects that TikTok provides. Alternatively, they can add special effects on their computer and upload that video into the app. The stop and start nature of the record button in TikTok has always allowed for playful practical effects as well.

TikTok has brought special effects back to its true intention—wowing people and telling funny and interesting stories.

 ## #MyResume

Use the in-app Green Screen Effect. Sure, it's not perfect. It can be fuzzy around the edges, and sometimes you disappear altogether—but that is precisely the charm. All you have to do is upload an image that becomes your background.

So what can you do with this effect? Anything! One TikTok user uploaded their resume to the green screen effect, then danced in front of it to the tune of "Roxanne." She tagged the @washingtonpost on TikTok. Her inventive use of the Green Screen Effect paid off and she got the job. (True story!)

 ## #GiftedNose

Use the nose painting effect. This in-app TikTok effect tracks your nose, "painting" the trail it leaves behind. Tapping the screen temporarily stops the tracking until you tap again and continue your masterpiece. I've spend HOURS painting with my nose, trying to write a message coherently.

 ## #RandomWiki

The Green Screen Effect can jumpstart any idea and turn it into something bigger. If you're feeling adventurous, hit "random wiki page" until an image appears. Create a TikTok that uses this image in the background.

#TwoOfMe

Duplicate yourself, using a simple editing trick. First, make sure your phone is in a stable position. A small phone tripod is best. Next, walk into the left side of the frame and give a wave. Now walk to the right side and wave as well. Make sure you have created enough distance so the two "yous" don't overlap.

In an editing program, separate the right-side waving and left-side waving footage into two segments. Now, "stack" the footage on top of itself. Cut out part of the top clip. It doesn't matter which clip is on top, so long as your left side and right side twin did not overlap. The best way to cut out is with the "masking tool." But, for beginners, let's just try the "crop" tool for now. Crop the top clip far enough to reveal your twin waving underneath.

And that's it! Now you have your twins, both on screen, waving back at you, as if there has always been two versions of you. Want more? Try triplets or quadruplets. It's tough to do, but always rewarding. It's easier than actually having quadruplets.

#NowYouSeeMeNowYouDont

Do a similar cloning effect to the previous prompt but actually allow yourself to disappear into thin air. Right-side Twin can walk to the left, but this time the left side is just an empty room. Have some fun with appearing and reappearing at will.

#PerfectLoopTaco

Create a "perfect loop." This is when the last moment of the TikTok moves seamlessly into the beginning of the TikTok. Let's say a TikTok starts and I'm halfway through eating a taco. I finish the taco, then there's a reaction shot from someone. Now, the camera cuts back to me eating the taco. As I get halfway through the taco, the TikTok starts over. I am now forever on loop, eating a new taco over and over again.

Here's the order:

1. I'm halfway through the first taco.

2. Reaction shot of friend, watching me eat the taco.

3. I start a second taco, and the TikTok ends when I'm halfway through the taco.

Your brain says, "Hey that's a perfect loop. He is eating tacos forever." The truth is, there's no real magic here. It's just a deceptive edit.

To create the loop, I shoot 1 after 3. So the shot list looks like:

2. Reaction shot of friend, watching me eat the taco.

3. I start a second taco, and the TikTok ends when I'm halfway through the taco.

1. I'm halfway through the first taco.

Shot 3 and 1 is one take. I simply take the shot, cut it in half, and place the second half at the top of the sequence. The second shot in the sequence is key as it provides a cutaway so I can create the loop.

#ProfessionalGreenScreen

Use actual green screen fabric to place yourself in a movie scene. Maybe you're the last Avenger arriving on scene at the end of *Avengers: End Game*. Everyone else appears on screen in all their glory, then here you are ... TikTok Man! A superhero with the power to repeat himself every 15 seconds.

Once you have shot your superhero intro, take the footage to your computer for the easiest edit of your life. In iMovie, the effect is simply called "Green/Blue Screen." Tapping this button immediately takes out the green background and allows you to place an image or movie underneath.

#MotionTrackerEffect

Because TikTok uses only images to help us differentiate between effects, I must apply a name to an effect. Let's call this one the Motion Tracker Effect.

This effect tracks the face on screen as it moves any direction—always placing that face directly in the center of the video. The video quality is a little pixelated. But the effect itself more than makes up for this, following your face around like a dog tracks a treat. Make a TikTok using this effect.

#RAGEEEEEE

Use the "Shake" effect to create a moment filled with rage. Try using it for only part of the TikTok so it's emphasized when on screen. It might be a back-and-forth between a calm person (no effect) and a person filled with rage (shake effect).

#JustInCase

Use the Incoming Call in-app TikTok effect to make a fake Facetime call. Some creators have used this effect to create a call featuring a one-sided conversation in which someone responds to you saying that you are on your way home. In one example of this, an actual dad on TikTok "calls" the user and allows them brief moments to respond to his questions.

These TikToks are intended to help people in case they find themselves in a scary situation. It creates the impression that someone is expecting you, and it could help keep away unwanted strangers or threats. Create your own version of this useful TikTok, and you might just help someone stay safe.

 #ImSerious

Pretend to be making a very serious TikTok. Then use this effect to undermine your serious tone:

 #StarWarsEpisodeX

Use the in-app "Star Wars Scroll" effect to tell a story while you just sit there in front of the camera. Let the text scroll across your face. In my experience, the less expressive your face, the funnier the effect. Don't forget to use *Star Wars*™ music!

#PracticalEffects

Play with perspective. Place a coffee mug at the foreground of a shot. Standing on a surface several feet behind the cup, "jump into" the coffee cup. Extra credit if you shake the table the mug is on so the coffee spills out as you jump in.

323 #PartyOfSix

Make a TikTok using the in-app crowd effect. This effect is easy to use, visually funny and even comes in a few varieties. One version clones the camera subject in a v-shape formation. Another version of this creates dozens of your clones, rolling past the screen, essentially marching forward onto the screen.

Let's say you're making a TikTok from the perspective of a host or hostess trying to seat a party of six.

The Host: Hello, how many for your table?

Table of people *(using the v-shape formation multiplying effect)*: Oh just five of us.

The Host: Excellent, follow me this way.

Table of people *(now using the effect with dozens of people)*: Okay!

The Host looks on in horror.

This crowd effect is perfect for a punchline, or even just added punctuation, at the end of any TikTok. It's also ideal when creating a TikTok that you are shooting by yourself without access to a crowd of people.

#TexasSwitch

Perform the "cowboy switch," also known as the "Texas switch." This is a movie effect that's been around for a century. Traditionally, it involves a stuntman and an actor. The stuntman performs a difficult stunt, then without the camera cutting, the actor pops up in the stuntman's place. This creates the illusion that the actor themselves performed the stunt.

In the interest of not injuring the fine people reading this book, let's attempt a cowboy switch that will be impressive, but not actually dangerous. You'll need two people who look moderately alike, wearing identical outfits. They will be Person 1.0 and Person 1.5. The possibilities are endless but I'll provide an easy example to get you started.

Have Person 1.0 point to something far away—the top window of a three-story house, for instance. After pointing they run out of shot as fast as they can toward the front door. As the camera pans up, Person 1.5 appears at the window pretending to be Person 1.0, as if they ran up the stairs in seconds.

For added difficulty, throw a ball high into the air, run into the house, and have Person 1.5 at the window catch it.

#WholeAgain

Use the Slide Block Puzzle in-app effect. The moment this effect begins recording, you are scrambled into nine pieces. After blinking, the effect unscrambles your screen and rearranges you into a whole human again.

#QuidditchCaptain

Fly around on a broom. This is normally achieved on TikTok by jumping up in the air and recording the exact millisecond you and the broom are airborne. That's fun, but requires a steady hand hitting record at the exact airborne moment forty times in a row. Instead, use an editing app to make this flying TikTok really impressive.

In one continuous take, record yourself jumping up in the air several times, moving a few inches forward with every jump. Then in your editing program, cut out the non-airborne moments. Within minutes, you'll have a seamless video of you flying through the air, ready to join a Quidditch team.

#DunDunDunDun

The Shark Attack in-app effect is a surprisingly beautiful effect, reflecting the top half of the screen onto the bottom to create an ocean of water. As a bonus, TikTok also included a shark fin circling your head ominously. This is prime opportunity for a funny caption using the text editor.

For example, a shark could be circling my head, while I follow its fin fearfully with my eyes. The text on screen: "Me watching the deadline for this book quickly approaching."

#PlantGrowth

Take a five-second shot of the plant every day from the same position. After a month or more, line the footage up in sequential order in your editing software, then speed it up by at least 10x. The plant will grow before your very eyes!

#StopMotionLEGO

Create a stop-motion TikTok. You'll need a firm place to hold your phone, such as a tripod, and a setting where the lighting is not likely to change as you record.

LEGO® pieces are great for stopmotion films because they are easy to move around. Your story could involve two LEGO minifigures walking toward each other.

Hit record on your phone and move the minifigures one step at a time. After each step, get out of frame so the camera can capture them without your fingers in the way. Continue to move the figures. Maybe they hug! Maybe they high-five! Maybe they just stare at each other. You're the storyteller here.

Then use an editing program to splice together each "movement." If you cut these moments up into small milliseconds, it will appear as if they're walking.

#CandyBarFingers

Use the Magic Wand in-app effect to cast a spell on someone. Wave your wand at someone and they turn into a candy bar that you bite into. Allow the candy bar to talk, pleading for you to change them back. After you've taken a bite, return them to human form. Now they're missing a finger. Le Fin.

#FirstDateStory

The Heart Bubbles in-app effect adds a pink filter and surrounds your face with heart-shaped bubbles. Use it to tell the story of a date or crush you had. Go back and forth between two people, using the effect on just one person to show a one-sided infatuation. Or perhaps the heart bubbles suddenly disappear at the moment the date loses its shine.

#EditedDance

The couple behind the account @happykelli, Kelli and Freeman, used a complicated effect for their first ever TikTok, which soon became very popular. You will need to employ some editing skills for this one, so to illustrate, I made a how-to TikTok about this on my personal page @davejorgenson.

First, dance in front of the camera to a song of your choice. Make big flashy moves on the beat or at big moments in the song. These will emphasize the effect later.

Next, take this footage into your editing program and mark the moments you want body parts to "connect." Grab screenshots of these moments and bring them into the program. Now, cut out a body part from the image. It could be a hand, leg, or arm. Once you have done this for every moment you marked before, bring these images back into your editing program.

Once the images are there, bring them into the timeline, at the exact moment they were cut from. Working backward, map them out to fly into the screen at the moment they collide with their body part.

In some cases, people have taken fifty or more body parts in just one TikTok!

INTERVIEW WITH

OLIVIA VAN FOXFACE
(@OliviaVanFoxface)

Dave Tell me about the Olivia Van Foxface account.

OVF I created my own little weird niche. At first I started doing millennial problems TikToks. A couple of those went pretty big, so I got to around 30,000 followers without showing many animals. Then [I found] being online was making me stressed. For two months, I didn't even look at TikTok. We had chickens and two llamas [on our farm]. That's what brings me joy. So I thought, I'm gonna just make little snippets of me saying hi to them in the morning. And then one of those videos just blew up.

Dave How many animals do you have?

OVF I've got three dogs now. Three cats, because they had a baby. A pig. Five goats. Four llamas. Two regular-sized horses, two miniature horses. Twelve ducks. Two geese. Two turkeys. And some chickens, too.

Dave What percentage of your farm would you say you document for TikTok?

OVF I don't document anything that has to do with the health of my animals, and I also don't give health advice.

Dave That makes sense. I don't want to distill your TikTok to just one thing, but it's bringing joy through all these different animals. You're not necessarily trying to give advice. You're just bringing happiness.

"I thought, I'm gonna just make little snippets of me saying hi to [my animals] in the morning. And then one of those videos just blew up."

OVF Exactly. That's what I try to keep it as. We're gonna just be stupid and I'm going to dance around like an idiot and make voices for 'em.

Dave Are you recording in-app or are you editing clips together later?

OVF It depends on what I'm doing. I would say 90 percent of what I do is in-app. And shooting with animals—everybody's constantly saying, "Make a video of this!" as if I can just tell the llama to sit down. What people don't realize is they just go sniff the camera and knock it over. If I want to get a video [I have to] put food over here so they are distracted.

Dave What's the number one thing that makes it so difficult to shoot with animals?

OVF They don't listen. They're all very entitled, which is why I call them "jerks" in my videos. It's endearing. I love them, but they are the worst. Champion will always bite you every time you're out there. Shadow just acts like I don't even exist.

Dave What's the TikTok that's made you say, "Why is this one viral?"

OVF Hands down, Mr. Pig when he was tiny. It's that song that goes "bounce that booty like a basketball." He's just shaking his butt, scratching it on a chair.

Dave Do you think it was the music choice?

OVF I think it was the combination. It's short, which obviously we know is much more shareable. It's something that anyone could send to their friends to go, "Oh my gosh, this is funny!" There's no context that you have to understand. It was just a tiny pig bouncing its butt to a funny song. The thing is, if you go viral, it's cool to have a million people see your video, but it's way more important to have a hundred people who will follow you anywhere. What sets me apart from other TikTokers is that my fan base is the most loyal and consistent and it's the same people.

Dave Can you give us an animal-based TikTok prompt?

OVF If you have an animal, give it a continued day-to-day storyline. Plan it out with a storyboard. That's the next plan for Mr. Pig. We're going to podcast the Adventures of Mr. Pig.

ANIMAL TIKTOKS

We simply cannot ignore the importance of pets and animals on the Internet. Cute animal videos will never disappear—and why would they? They're the only truly pure thing on the Internet that everybody agrees on.

Fighting with your aunt over politics? Post a dog pic. Can't believe your brother posted THAT article? Let off steam by uploading a video of your cat chasing a string. And so, this book ends how the Internet began, swarming in animal memes.

#CountyFairJudging

Go to a county or state fair. Find a barn of animals and rate each of them based on arbitrary things.

"This goat has great skin! He must moisturize."

"He is quieter than the rest. He must be a Pisces."

You know, stuff like that.

#TextToSpeechDog

Record a voice for an animal but this time type the "dialogue" into a text-to-speech tool. Record on your phone while your computer plays the dialogue.

You might show your dog by the door, staring at you, saying in a robot voice:

"I love going outside and I hope we go outside soon again. It has been five minutes since we last went outside and I saw a squirrel and another dog and then a squirrel and a cat and then we came back inside. Is it time to go outside again yet?"

#AnimalsCanSpeak

If you have an animal that you've given a voice, record them "talking" to camera. Olivia Van Foxface has a running joke with a pig called Harry Plopper Spider Pig. His voice is hysterical and we hope Harry Plopper Spider Pig never leaves TikTok.

#RatRace

Race mice through a maze, if you have a mice ... and a maze. And cheese.

#BopItPet

Use the "Bop It Challenge" audio but with an animal. For the uninitiated, "Bop It!" is a popular game in which kids pull, twist, and "bop" a toy as it calls out the demands. If you don't pull, twist, or bop in time, you lose. This could be extremely cute with an animal, especially when you (gently) bop them on the nose. You should maybe substitute "pet" and "give a belly rub" for the twist and pull commands, though.

#KittensUnboxed

Challenge someone not to smile and then reveal an open box of kittens. I pity the person who can hold back a smile when faced with a box full of adorable kittens.

#ClassyDogDinner

Give your dog a romantic candle-lit dinner. Put your dog in a suit jacket and set a place for them at a fancy table, with a plate of dog food in front of them. Play some classical music in the background to really set the scene.

#LadyAndTheTikTok

Put two dogs in front of a plate of spaghetti and play the song from *Lady and the Tramp*. Record what happens.

#WhyImVegan

If you're a vegan or vegetarian, make a TikTok explaining why. Is it for health reasons or for the animals or both?

#EggUnboxed

If you have the memory, battery power, patience, and egg, set up your phone or camera to record an egg hatching. In the same TikTok or in a series, show the growth of the young chick (or reptile!) as it grows into an adult.

#MyPetFoodRecommendation

Make a TikTok recommending cat or dog food (for a pet).

#AntFarmLife

Buy an ant farm and keep track of the ants' progress. Report back every day to let everyone know what the ants are up to and if they're still farming.

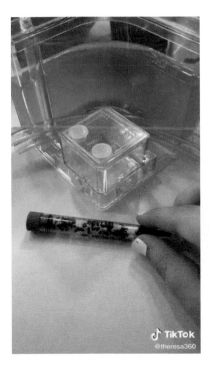

Follow for
✦ Ant Updates ✦

♪ TikTok
@theresa360

♪ TikTok
@theresa360

#MisunderstoodAnimals

Make a TikTok about a misunderstood animal. Pigeons get a bad rap, even though their ancestors were expertly bred to carry messages—and they were pretty adept at it! They deserve some credit.

#CarrotChomp

Feed your rabbit a carrot. Put a microphone or another phone really close to it and record the audio while they're eating, so the world can hear the adorable sounds of a rabbit happily chewing on a carrot.

#SharkMisconceptions

Make a TikTok about common mistakes people make about sharks. Some are dangerous, yes. But most are not.

The movie *Jaws* really hurt the reputation of sharks. That said, the audio of the *Jaws* theme playing in the background while you're explaining how most sharks won't hurt you is a little dig at the movie that misrepresented them.

#DogTrainingTips

Make some dog-training TikToks!

If you are a dog trainer or have mastered a particular aspect of dog training, demonstrate this on TikTok. If it's not clear from the prompts so far, this author has a somewhat new dog and has spent countless hours watching leash training, trick training, and any other type of training tips on TikTok accounts run by dog trainers. People will never stop having dogs, so the need for dog-training TikToks is endless.

#PetForAPet

Record your cat as you are petting it. Make sure they are purring contentedly. Abruptly stop petting your cat and put their paw on your hand and ask them to pet you back.

#FrogCheckIn

If you have wildlife in your neighborhood, visit your local animal/s every day. Maybe you have stray cats in your neighborhood, or a rabbit family slowly destroying your garden, or even a frog that frequents your pond. Checking in on those animals and recording your one-sided conversation with them is prime Animal TikTok material.

#WhaleCaptions

Speak whale. Look up "whale song" online and try to mimic their calls. Include subtitles to show what the whale is saying.

#RabbitBeat

If you have a rabbit, get a stethoscope and put it over your pet's heart. Record the audio of their heart beating rapidly. Set it to a song with an equally quick tempo, such as a very fast-paced trap or metal song.

#CatnipBliss

Give a cat catnip. Record the results. Choose an appropriate song from TikTok's library to accompany your video. Make sure it is the responsible amount of catnip.

#IAmABird

Record yourself listening to different bird sounds and trying to repeat them with your own whistling or squawks.

#ADayOnTheFarm

If you're a farmer, show your day-to-day life. What time do you wake up? How long are you out working? Do your animals have different names and personalities? What's it like saying goodbye to an animal? Answer as many questions as you can, because you will get tons of questions in the comments.

#HalfDogHalfHuman

Put your dog or cat on your shoulders and then don a large trench coat or lab coat, with their head sticking out. As long as they are comfortable, walk around and greet people. Introduce yourself as your pet's name and try to shake their hand.

#CatWalk

If your pet is happy to be dressed up, take inspiration from Rover the cat and show off your pet's unique style with a pet fashion show.

#CowMilking101

Show how to properly milk a cow. Sing to the cow while you're milking it because this is TikTok and cows deserve music too.

#DogHeaven

Pretend you work on the farm where all the dogs were sent to "go live upstate" when they suddenly disappeared from our childhood homes.

"Hello, I work at the farm where dogs go away sometimes. I can't show you your dog right now because it's playing with all the other dogs, but I'm happy to report they arrived here at the farm and are thoroughly enjoying themselves!"

#SquirrelTalk

Conduct a professional interview with a squirrel. Ask them a number of questions and chase them around the park as if they are a source in a story and are trying to get away from you.

But you are a determined reporter. You need to know if the squirrel knows about the missing nuts in the area and may know the people connected to this crime. Why hasn't the squirrel spoken up about this? Are they hiding something? The people of the park deserve to know.

Dress up for the interview, as if this is a huge story going live on national television. This could be your big break—if you can get the squirrel to talk.

#FollowForAFish

If you have a fish tank, encourage your followers to name them. Every TikTok, introduce one of your fish and describe its personalities, interests, motivations, and career goals. Ask people to comment with a name for the fish. Pick your favorite name and then use the video reply function to let the user know the fish is now named after them and they are officially the TikTok Fish Godparent of this fish.

Make videos that check in with the fish over time and let their sponsors know what they are up to. Hopefully your followers will become very attached and build a whole community around these fishies.

#VetVisitDiary

Record your pet's trip to the vet. Provide audio of what the pet is thinking, like a diary. This audio can go over a video montage of the animal in the car, arriving, getting a shot, and leaving.

Dear Diary,

We went back to The Bad Place again. I was made to believe it was a road trip, but we quickly took the turn down the road to The Bad Place. I had promised myself I would never return, but Master seemed intent on making this journey once again. Quickly, I found myself on The Forbidden Table again, humiliated. Master watched as The Unholy One poked me with a sharp Death Needle and smiled like nothing terrible was happening. Shortly after we left, I made sure to urinate everywhere to express my disgust with The Bad Place.

Find a violin track on TikTok and have it play softly in the background for extra drama.

#WasntMe

Use the song "It Wasn't Me" by Shaggy and show your animal and some mischief they have created. They may be standing among the wreckage of a couch they destroyed.

#PuppyToDog

If you've adopted a new animal, a puppy for instance, get them to sit next to an easily recognizable object that will allow people to understand the size of the dog.

Every week record your puppy sitting in the same position, next to your chosen object, for just a few seconds. Edit all that footage together into a puppy-growing-up montage. I wish I had done this for my puppy. Now, you must do it instead.

#CatsAndDogsTogether

If you happen to have a dog and a cat that like each other, record them hanging out. Sit back and watch as millions of people like your video.

Editor Rosie Peet
Designer Anita Mangan
Project Art Editor Jenny Edwards
Senior Designer Lauren Adams
Production Editor Marc Staples
Production Controller Lloyd Robertson
Managing Editor Paula Regan
Managing Art Editor Jo Connor
Publishing Director Mark Searle

DK would like to thank the author Dave Jorgenson, Catherine Saunders
for additional editing, Bianca Hezekiah for authenticity review, Heather Wilcox
for proofreading, and Jo Lightfoot for commissioning the project.

From the author: Thanks to my super-secret intern Liz for helping me track down half the
creator interviews, Hannah for explaining how books work, Michelle for her constant
cheerleading, Rosie for letting me miss my fake deadlines, and my family for accepting weird
things I pursue without too many questions. And most of all, thanks to Mariana for constant
love and support—it must be exhausting.

First American Edition, 2021
Published in the United States by DK Publishing
1450 Broadway, Suite 801, New York, New York 10018

A catalog record for this book is available from the Library of Congress.

ISBN 978-0-7440-3992-4

DK books are available at special discounts when purchased in bulk for
sales promotions, premiums, fund-raising, or educational use.
For details, contact: DK Publishing Special
Markets, 1450 Broadway, Suite 801, New York, New York 10018
SpecialSales@dk.com

Printed and bound in China

For the curious

www.dk.com